TRADESMEN OF ST. CROIX

U.S. VIRGIN ISLANDS

KAREN C. THURLAND

authorHOUSE®

AuthorHouse™
1663 Liberty Drive
Bloomington, IN 47403
www.authorhouse.com
Phone: 1 (800) 839-8640

Published by AuthorHouse 12/31/2018

ISBN: 978-1-5462-5690-8 (sc)
ISBN: 978-1-5462-5689-2 (hc)
ISBN: 978-1-5462-5688-5 (e)

Library of Congress Control Number: 2018910026

Print information available on the last page.

Cover Photo: Will A. Thurland demonstrates chair caning at the 1990 Smithsonian Folklife Festival.
Courtesy of the Ralph Rinzler Folklife Archives and Collections, Center for Folklife and Cultural Heritage, Smithsonian Institution.

This book is printed on acid-free paper.

DEDICATION

This book is dedicated to my father Will A. Thurland, a joiner, carpenter and jack of all trades. He was also a teacher, musician, band director, soldier and culture bearer. His guiding words to me over the years were "Always Do Your Best."

ACKNOWLEDGEMENTS

I am extremely grateful to the people who contributed their time, stories and assistance with the development of this book. Thanks to Anne Thurland, Gerard Doward, Celeste Knight Lang, Josephine Hector, Maurice Thomas and Carol Wakefield for their review of the manuscript and their valuable suggestions. Special thanks to Anne Thurland for the layout of the book and the photo restoration. Thanks to the St. Croix Landmarks Society and Our Town Frederiksted. A sincere thanks to Roberta Knowles, Ed. D. for her editing work.

The Virgin Islands Transfer Centennial Commission is a major sponsor of this project.

CONTENTS

LIST OF PHOTOGRAPHS

INTRODUCTION

M y interest in writing about a few notable tradesmen on St. Croix began when I started conducting genealogical research and noticed the various occupational trades present on the island during the Danish period, and I also found new information about the goldsmiths/silversmiths in my family. Those Thurland family members, from the 1820s to 1913, were listed as goldsmiths and silversmiths. The Thurland family has been known to be cabinetmakers and joiners during the twentieth century, but my father Will A. Thurland told me about the goldsmiths in the family and the fact that his father Peter G. Thurland Sr. broke away from the goldsmith tradition and decided that he would make fine furniture.

The Ancestor Discovery Group held a genealogical exhibit in 2007, at the Florence Williams Public Library, and for my family's display I listed the tradesmen in my family. That event further sparked my interest in researching and collecting pertinent information about tradesmen on St. Croix and writing on that topic for interested readers and future generations of Virgin Islanders.

My research about St. Croix's tradesmen continued to grow when I found out that two silver spoons made by George Thurland, my great-great-great-grandfather, were housed at the Danish National Museum. It was an indescribable experience when my sister Anne and I traveled to Denmark in 2009 and were allowed to see and hold the silverware that was made by one of the goldsmiths in our family. Those spoons were crafted over 150 years ago in the 1800s and were still in mint condition. Anne and I felt a deep sense of pride and excitement when we held the silver spoons in our gloved-hands. When we turned over the spoons we saw his trademark initials – GT- and the cross he engraved, which represented the island of St. Croix.

It intrigued me that those spoons were made in the nineteenth century, and I was holding them in the twenty-first century. What had started out as a historical research inquiry became a personal journey as I discovered additional relatives who earned a living as Free Colored tradesmen and the fact that their works can still be seen today, several generations later.

Tradesmen are commonly referred to as artisans or craftsmen, but here in the Virgin Islands tradesmen is the most popular term. Their creations were made with hand tools and required skill, creativity, patience and long hours to finish. Materials were scarce in the islands, so they did a lot of improvising to complete their work, and the items that were ordered from Europe or the United States took time to be shipped to the island.

Tradesmen were a vital part of the islands' economic activities from early Danish settlement days. The plantation owners and townspeople needed masons, carpenters, blacksmiths, wheelwrights, joiners, tailors, shoemakers and several other artisans. Tradesmen from Denmark, Norway, other European countries, and nearby Caribbean islands came to St. Croix to find opportunities in their craft. Enslaved men who learned a trade were sometimes hired out to other plantations and saved enough money to buy their own freedom and that of family members. The trade was passed on to their children, many who became part of the growing free colored population on the island during the era of Danish enslavement.

According to the book *Arts in the U.S. Virgin Islands*, "Characteristic of the past was a great pride in workmanship. Coopers, wheelwrights, tanners, saddlers and tailors were among many whose trades passed from father to son."

Tradesmen passed down their techniques and knowledge to their children, and that tradition remained on St. Croix until roughly the 1960s when the population increased and the demand for various articles to be readily available led to the importation of fabricated goods made off-island. Tradesmen could not provide articles in large quantities or on a timely basis. They operated small businesses and could not keep up with the number of requests for handmade articles like gold or silver jewelry, mahogany furniture or tailored clothing.

These men took an active role in their respective churches, served on civic and religious committees and also made financial contributions to those institutions. Crucian tradesmen engaged in many community activities and provided positive guidance to island youngsters by organizing musical bands, festival troupes and sports activities. They were highly respected throughout the island and served as role models for many young men.

Their workshops became places for political commentary and local gossip. Politicians stopped in the shops to talk and to mingle with people. I remember politicians from both St. Croix and St. Thomas stopping by my grandfather's workshop in the late afternoons and conversing on the major issues of the day. I met many politicians when I went into the workshop to deliver a telephone message to my grandfather Peter or my uncle Bertie. Of course, I could not stay in the workshop for any length of time because it was considered too dangerous for children to be around the machines and the ever present smell of sawdust.

Since the U. S. Virgin Islands observed the 2017 Centennial of the transfer of the islands from Denmark to the United States of America, it is important to note that three of the tradesmen in this book witnessed the transfer of the Danish West Indies to the United States on March 31, 1917, in Christiansted. Peter G. Thurland Sr. and Alfonso S. Forbes participated in the transfer ceremony when they played in the Christiansted Industrial Brass Band during the 4:00 p.m. afternoon ceremony. Carlos H. McGregor observed the lowering of the Danish flag (the Danneborg) and the raising of the American flag at Fort Christiansvaern that same afternoon. Along with his father Charles Robert McGregor, a master tailor, Carlos helped make the uniforms for the Industrial Brass Band for that very special occasion.

The tradesmen in this book are examples of some of the finest Black artisans on St. Croix, who came from a tradition of sons following in their fathers' footsteps. The men in this book are but a few of the many talented tradesmen who lived and worked on the island.

Arthur Abel was a joiner and builder from Frederiksted, who learned his trade from his father. They worked on many buildings in that town and did the gingerbread decorations for many buildings. Abel worked for the Department of Public Works for over 50 years and was affectionately known as "Mr. Public Works."

Monroe F. Clendenin, a goldsmith from Christiansted, worked in that trade for over 70 years. He learned his craft from his father and at a very young age opened his own shop. Monroe was active in the community with his Pirates of Penzance Festival Troupe comprised of young men from the various neighborhoods of Christiansted. This tall man was also known for his individual entry in the annual festival parades.

Hugo "Nookie" Doyle from Christiansted was one of the last blacksmiths in the Caribbean. Nookie learned the trade from his father and opened his own shop. He was also a farrier who trained and cared for horses.

Alfonso S. Forbes learned about shoemaking from his father and opened his own shop at the young age of 16. He developed an interest in music, played in a local brass band, served in the U. S. Navy Band, and later was bandmaster for his own band and became known as the "March King." He worked as an accountant, real estate appraiser, and even tried his hand at painting landscapes.

Carlos H. McGregor, a tailor and my maternal great-uncle, learned his trade from his father, and together they made uniforms for Danish officials, policemen, and some of the leading citizens of Christiansted. Carlos, in his leisure time, played with the Christiansted Cricket Club as its batsman. Mr. McGregor gave us a vivid account of life in Christiansted town during the Danish period and the early years of American rule.

Halver L. Moolenaar, from St. Thomas, learned the mason trade from his Uncle George in St. Thomas. His block-laying skills are legendary, and he was known as a mason and general contractor who constructed many houses on St. Croix and St. Thomas.

Peter Horatio Thurland, a goldsmith and my paternal great-great-great-uncle, was born free in 1832 and probably learned the trade from his father George Thurland. Peter worked in both Christiansted and in Charlotte Amalie, St. Thomas.

Peter Gregory Thurland Sr., my paternal grandfather, was a cabinetmaker and bandmaster. He broke the family tradition of goldsmithing by becoming a cabinetmaker. Peter opened his own shop and taught the building and repair of mahogany furniture to his sons and many young men who came to learn the trade as apprentices. He loved music and played in local brass bands, served in the U.S. Navy Band from 1917 to 1921, and organized the St. Croix Community Band, which provided free concerts in both towns and in Grove Place. He passed on both traditions to my father Will, my uncles, two brothers and two cousins who today repair and restore mahogany furniture.

The names of men involved in the various trades, from the early 1800s to 1911, can be obtained from the Virgin Islands Social History Associates (VISHA) website. Other valuable sources of information such as Danish Census records, Free Colored lists, land matrikels (cadastral records), and church records can be viewed at the VISHA website and at the research library at the Estate Whim Museum. The research library at Whim also has an extensive historic photo collection with images from Axel Ovesen and Andreas Lauridsen, both Danes, and other photographers.

The Danish government provided digitized copies of its collections from its archives, libraries and museums for the 2017 Centennial of the transfer of the islands to the United States. These resources can be accessed online, and they contain pertinent information that can assist in the interpretation and documentation of topics relevant to the people, culture and history of St. Croix. Historians and writers have advocated for these documents to be made available to Virgin Islanders. We now have access to various Virgin Islands records and must make use of those valuable resources. It is important for us to document our history for our understanding and that of future generations of Virgin Islanders.

This historical reader is my attempt to capture the creativity and ingenuity of local Black tradesmen who made a living with their hands and minds and in doing so made contributions to the cultural heritage of the island of St. Croix. I challenge others to research and write about their family or important people and document their accomplishments and describe the contributions they made to the history and culture of our beautiful island.

ARTHUR ABEL
JOINER

A rthur Abel, a joiner and builder, worked for the Department of Public Works on St. Croix for 54 years, insuring that the town of Frederiksted had water, its streets were paved, and all the government buildings were properly maintained. He made sure the Christmas lights were put up on the streets every year for the Christmas Festival celebrations. In fact, even after his retirement Abel volunteered at Public Works for ten years until his death. He was affectionately called "Mr. Public Works" by his many friends and employees.

Arthur Abel was born on September 17, 1902, in the town of Frederiksted, St. Croix, Danish West Indies to James Abel and Christophina Wren. He attended the Danish School, a public grammar school in Frederiksted, where his education ended when he completed Book Six, equivalent to a sixth grade education. After completing his education, he started working with his father "Boss" James at the age of 14 and also learned the joinery trade at the Public Works Department.

Arthur's son O'Neal Abel, in an interview, proudly stated, "My father was a carpenter, joiner and a 'jack of all trades.' He turned bed posts and newel posts in his shop, which was located on the ground floor of his home at No. 61 Hospital

Street in Frederiksted. He helped build the second floor of that house with his father James."

Arthur Abel made the spiral posts for the Frederiksted Bandstand and the columns for the Veteran's Memorial at Fort Christiansvaern in Christiansted. He made chalices of both dark and light mahogany and donated them to the priests at St. Patrick's Church. Abel was a Moravian and his sons become Moravians, but his daughters were baptized in the Catholic church.

Arthur Abel taught several joiners and carpenters in Frederiksted, such as Cyril Murphy. Norman Williams of Grove Place, father of Senator Patrick Williams, also worked with him.

The employees at Public Works who worked with Arthur Abel included Hubert McIntosh, chief mechanic, James Petersen, chief clerk, David Hamilton, carpenter and later inspector, and Alec Benjamin, blacksmith. Several other employees were "Hog Head," Edwin Thomas, Eugene Thomas, Vernon Clarke, Ralph Johnson Sr., and Alphonso Sackey, a carpenter.

At the Department of Public Works, Arthur Abel was in charge of the Frederiksted district and held the position of district superintendent for Frederiksted. He was responsible for all the projects and everything in Public Works west of Kingshill including the Kingshill's Poor Farm (the Herbert Grigg Home), the repair and maintenance of the police station at Kingshill, and was responsible for every government structure west of Kingshill. The hospital, the public

1. Arthur Abel
Courtesy of St. Croix Landmarks Society

grammar schools, the high school, the La Vallee School, and Fort Frederik all came under his purview. He built the old pavilion in the Terrence Martin Ball Park. He used his skills as a builder to oversee the successful completion, repair and maintenance of all those structures. The water wells in the town also came under his supervision, and he took care of the water system in Frederiksted and up to Estate LaVallee. Ivan Latimer learned the water system under Arthur Abel.

Arthur Abel put up the first Christmas Festival lights in Frederiksted. His son, O'Neal Abel, worked with his father at the Department of Public Works and remembers putting up those lights and making the street banners when governors came to Frederiksted. "Those large banners that hung across the streets were designed with stencils, painted, and then had triangular holes cut into them.

My father Arthur Abel built the old race track and maintained it. I built the new race track and dug every hole and planted every rail. He laid out the race track at Flamboyant Park, which was a six-furlong track built in the 1950s that replaced the Jerusalem race track."

O'Neal Abel explained, "The familiar shape of the island of St. Croix at the present Randall James Racetrack was my work. Manning's Bay was an old track. In Frederiksted, we had the Stoney Ground track.

My father's philosophy was that you put in an honest day's work. O'Neal Abel remembers when his father played tricks on some guys. "He saw them standing around idling on the job. My father told them to dig a hole to find a pipe, which was not there, and then made them cover the hole back up."

Lena A. Schulterbrandt, the daughter of Arthur Abel, recollects that her father loved driving cars, boat racing and horse racing. "As a matter of fact, he was a starter for the horse races. He sang in the choir at two churches: at Friedensberg Moravian, where he was a parishioner, and at the adjacent Holy Trinity Lutheran with his friend Darnley Petersen. She remembers men like Charlie Clarke and C.R.T. Brow meeting to talk in Abel's workshop, located underneath his house on Hospital Street. They most likely talked about local issues and politics."

Arol Abel, Arthur's grandson, remembers riding in his grandfather's truck as a young boy to deliver mahogany furniture to customers. Some of Abel's clients were Darnley Petersen, Alva McFarlane, Percy Gardine, the Merwins, and the Ayers at Beresford Manor. Arol also remembers that his grandfather made a mahogany bowl for the Queen of Denmark when she visited St. Croix in 1976.

Arthur Abel died in January 1985, at the age of 83, but has not been forgotten for his years of dedicated service to the Department of Public Works and to the people of St. Croix, particularly the town of Frederiksted. The refurbished Danish School in Frederiksted was dedicated in Abel's honor on September 26, 2009. The Arthur Abel Complex, now houses the governor's Frederiksted offices.

2. The Arthur Abel Complex in Frederiksted
Courtesy of Arol Abel

The woodworking shop of Arthur Abel has been relocated to a room below the Great House at the Estate Whim Museum. One of Abel's grandsons had donated the tools and several pieces of furniture to the museum. The Museum's website refers to him as a local carpenter who made a lot of the gingerbread decorative designs in nearby Frederiksted.

Arthur Abel's legacy of service continued with his son O'Neal, who also went to work for the Department of Public Works. O'Neal started at Public Works in 1953 and still has the payroll for his entry date. He remembers Sylvester "Blinky" McIntosh's name on that same payroll. O'Neal was on two payrolls for a while because he was on one job for three weeks and then on another payroll for another job.

O'Neal recalls, "Years ago the night soil (sewage) trucks and the pickup was under the jurisdiction of the Department of Public Works. The wages for that period was 81 cents an hour for a master tradesman, 61 cents an hour for a tradesman, 58 cents an hour for a trades' helper, and 40 cents an hour for a laborer.

When the ships came into Frederiksted, the workers left their jobs at Public Works and did stevedore work for Merwin Shipping Company for two days, all day and throughout the night. The men made more money there getting the bags of sugar loaded for shipment, and the Department of Public Works tolerated it."

O'Neal Abel and John Brady provided a compilation of names of Public Works employees and tradesmen. Brady's father was a chief maintenance mechanic responsible for the maintenance of the Federal Aviation Authority (FAA) buildings at the St. Croix airport. At that time the airport was supervised by La Bega Alexander, Victor Gibeon, and Albert "Bertie" Neltropp.

3. The Victoria House with Gingerbread Designs
Photo by Karen C. Thurland

O' Neal Abel and Brady, wanting to pass on the names of other tradespeople, gave the names that they remembered. The tradesmen from Frederiksted were Alec Benjamin, blacksmith; Jacob Bennerson, goldsmith and piano tuner; Chief Herman Sarauw, goldsmith; Johnny Wilson, shoemaker; Martinez, shoemaker; Levy Messer, boat builder; John Richards, mechanic; and Albert "Doc" Holiday, diver.

Al Franklin's father Joseph was a tinsmith, and he made cups. Back in those days, tinsmiths also made iceboxes and ovens for people. Sammy Stevens was also a tinsmith in Frederiksted. The electricians were Peter Derrick, Julio Delgado, Vincent Doward, and Halvor "Buddy" Berg, who was also a mechanic. The plumbers were Ohanio Holst and Aage Schou. The tailors were Norris Wyre and James "Jimmy" Hendricksen.

The Frederiksted fishermen who used a seine, a net with sinkers and floats, were Eugene Bennerson, Arthur Smith, and Archie Stevens. Several other fishermen were Joseph Prince, Zachariah Roberts, Albert Edwards, Alexander Michael, and Walter Huggins.

Arthur Abel's mahogany furniture can be found in homes on St. Croix along with his gingerbread designs on the exteriors of houses. Buildings he worked on can still be seen throughout the town of Frederiksted.

Monroe F. Clendenen
GOLDSMITH

M onroe Fermin Clendenen, a noted goldsmith, worked at his shop at No. 37 King Street in Christiansted, where he made earrings, bracelets, and chains out of gold or silver. He also repaired jewelry for his customers.

Monroe Clendenen was born on November 3, 1906, to James and Anna Victoria Loffler Clendenen in Christiansted on the island of St. Croix. His father James was a goldsmith and is listed in the 1911 Danish Census as a jeweler and residing at Nos. 65 and 66 East Street. Monroe, when he was seven years old, began learning the trade from his father as was the tradition of sons continuing the family trade. Monroe worked in that profession for over 60 years.

Will Thurland, the author's father, at the age of 11 was sent to work with Monroe Clendenen after his father Peter told him that his great uncle and great grandfathers were jewelers and it would be good if Will and his younger brother Pete learned that trade. As young apprentices, the brothers went to Monroe Clendenen's shop after school and on Saturdays. They received no pay working as apprentices as was the custom.

4. Monroe Clendenen at His Work Table
Courtesy of the St. Croix Landmarks Society

The goldsmith shop was located on King Street across from Joseph Alexander's Store, the Firm of John Alexander and next to Miss Heidi Rengger. The building had a couple of steps to go up. Monroe utilized the same workbench and stool his father James had used for his work and had given to Monroe to continue with the goldsmith trade. Inside the shop were the furnace, the flat bed, the hand-turn wheel, the swedge and other tools of the goldsmith's trade, such as the scale, the wire stretcher, and metal plates.

Will Thurland remembers turning a wheel as Monroe melted the gold and put it into something that looked like a lathe. Will and his brother Pete turned the wheel until the gold got to the desired thickness that Monroe wanted. He stated the following:

"We assisted Monroe when he melted gold or silver granules to make a liquid substance. Next, he put the liquid into a pot on a fire. It comes in strips, and he would put those strips on the wheel to get the exact thickness that he wanted. Then he would cut the strips to the desired length that was needed.

When making a ring, Monroe placed a strip on a cylinder and cut it according to the size of your finger. He would bend it to the size and sweat it, so the two ends could meet after being bent. Then he would solder it together and form the ring. Pete and I would polish the rings for Monroe's customers. We mostly polished the rings. That's what we did most of the time we were there. Monroe also made bracelets and earrings for people. Clan Jacobs, another Christiansted jeweler, used to work with Monroe but also did work for his own customers."

Monroe Clendenen Jr. remembered going to his father's shop on King Street near the home of Miss Heidi Rengger on the corner of King and Market Streets. Monroe Jr. used to pump the organ in Lutheran Church for her on Sundays. Monroe Jr. said that he did not learn the trade but his brother Austin tried to learn the trade, but he did not succeed in doing so.

Monroe Junior explained the process. "My father made earrings, bracelets, pins and rings. He made my confirmation ring, which I no longer have. I used to see him drawing wire to make bracelets. I used to turn the wheel for him when he was behind in his work. In his shop, he had a gauge with holes for the different ring sizes. I have seen him melt the stuff and put it on a block to shape and cool. He never polished his jewelry with a cloth; instead he used some twine.

I remember one Saturday I went to the shop to get the groceries because my father did the shopping for the house. I don't recall why, but he made me sit on a chair in punishment. He had a lot of work for the people from the country and had not finished it. On Saturdays, people from the countryside came to town to shop for groceries and clothing. A lady came into the shop and asked me, 'Where is your father?'

Since I was in punishment, I wanted to get even with him, so I said, 'He said to tell you that he gone out. I then pointed to the backroom where he was. The lady went after him and gave him a piece of her mind. Then, he came after me. So I said to him, 'I told her what you had told me to tell her.' But, I still received a punishment from him.

My father was very artistic and he put his own style into the jewelry he made. He had that old Danish handwriting that he put into his work. The jewelry business started diminishing with the availability of costume jewelry. Older people would buy my father's jewelry but young people bought costume jewelry."

Monroe Clendenen Sr. hosted several traditional "Old Year's Night dances" at the Congressional Hall on Church Street in Christiansted. People looked forward to this annual social event. Will Thurland remembers people walking to the dance after the midnight church service. They left the Lutheran, Catholic and Moravian churches after the midnight service and walked to the dancehall. Men wore jackets and ties, while the women had on their nice dresses. Will played his saxophone at several of those dances with the Jive Bombers Orchestra. He said the Liebert Orchestra also played at some of the Old Year's dances. This was during the

1930s when the bands played waltzes, the foxtrots and quelbe' music. The dances were held annually until the 1940s, when a large number of men left to join the U. S. military during the Second World War.

In the 1952 Christmas Festival parade, Monroe Clendenen stepped out as the Grand Marshall. Clendenen organized a masquerade troupe that became known as the Pirates of Penzance. Dressed in pirate garb, complete with black eye patch and sword, Clendenen was definitely a crowd pleaser. His troupe performed on the Christiansted wharf, throughout the island, and in the annual Christmas Festival parades. Monroe was over six feet tall and led his group of pirates down the streets of town. Many young men participated in this troupe.

When Monroe no longer had his pirate troupe, he entered the parade as an individual entry. Ruth Moore wrote in the *Arts in the U.S. Virgin Islands* publication, "Mr. Clendenen led the festival parade on St. Croix in 1965. He no longer dressed as a pirate but in top hat and tails."

Mrs. Leola Carroll, wife of legislator Eric Carroll, remembered Monroe dressed as Uncle Sam in the parades. The author, as a young girl, also remembers Monroe Clendenen dressed in red, white and blue clothing, with his top hat, making his way down King Street in Christiansted in a festival parade.

Clendenen was a big horse-racing fan and went to many of the local races. He supported the St. Croix Turf Club, which sponsored several races, and was a starter for several races.

Brian Bishop, founder of Crucian Gold, visited Monroe when he was sick in the hospital. Brian stated, "In the early 1970s, I was just beginning my career as a metalsmith. I had already designed the flower of life, the abstract butterfly, the twisted Ankh, and perfected the authentic hand-tied metal 'turkshead.' The 'Crucian Bracelet,' which is identified by the knot button latch, had not been designed as yet.

At that time, my mother, Rosemary Petre Bishop, was a nurse at the Charles Harwood Memorial Hospital in Richmond, and Monroe was a patient. Now my mother was the quintessential nurse with an amazing bedside manner, who spared no effort to ease patients' suffering and to divert them sometime. Her choice of diversion this time was to invite me in and introduce me to Mr. Monroe Clendenen.

We ended up having a delightful conversation. The one thing I remember was Monroe went into quite some detail about his technique for making the prototype for what was I believe the earliest rendition of a metal sugar mill as a piece of jewelry. It was probably more than a decade later that I designed what I named the Crucian Mill, featuring the old tree waving like a flag victorious over the evils of the sugar industry 250 years ago. Monroe died very shortly after our encounter, and I always wished I could have had a much longer relationship with the man as he was clearly a Crucian treasure."

5. The Congressional Council Hall at No. 17 Church Street in Christiansted Monroe Clendenen held his Old Year's dances here.

Photo by Jack Delano   Library of Congress

6. The Pirates of Penzance Festival Troupe Led by Monroe Clendenen
Courtesy of the St. Croix Landmarks Society

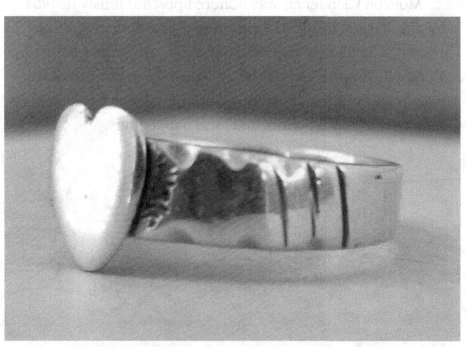

7. A Ring Made by Monroe Clendenen
Monique Clendinen Watson got this ring as a present
from her grandmother Everitta Clendinen on her 13th
birthday in November 1972. Monroe Clendinen was a
cousin and one of the last goldsmiths on St. Croix.
Courtesy of Monique Clendinen Watson

Monroe Clendenen, at the age of 70, died on May 5, 1977, at the Charles Harwood Hospital in Christiansted. His funeral service was held at the Lord God of Sabaoth Lutheran Church, and he was laid to rest in the Christiansted Cemetery.

Monroe Clendenen was honored posthumously in 1984 by the Virgin Islands Legislature. According to Bill No. 15-0947, Clendenen was referred to as an "Ambassador of Goodwill" for the Virgin Islands. The Bill further stated that friends and visitors would drop into Clendenen's goldsmith shop to talk about politics and local happenings.

Hugo "Nookie" Doyle
MASTER BLACKSMITH

H ugo "Nookie" Doyle was born on February 23, 1922, in Christiansted, St. Croix to Rudolph Doyle and Marie Samuel. His father, a blacksmith, passed that trade on to his son. Nookie attended St. Mary's Catholic School and worked with his father after school, on weekends and during the summer months.

Rudolph Doyle's blacksmith shop was located at Bassin Triangle, where the former Legislature of the Virgin Islands building stands today. Joseph Foy, known as Master Wow, was the other blacksmith, who also had a shop in that area.

Richard Schrader Sr. in his book, *Under de Taman Tree,* wrote that Nookie worked in the shop handing his father various tools or helped the other men hold a horse, mule or donkey's foot while "Boss Doyle" fitted and nailed a shoe on the animal. Nookie told Schrader that he liked to operate the bellows which pushed the air into the forge turning up the flames on a piece of iron, making it red hot. His father then plucked the iron out with long tongs and hammered it into shape on the anvil.

Schrader wrote, "Nookie along with his father repaired the wheels for phaetons and carts. They made parts for ploughs, hoes, cane bills, machetes, and other field tools on a large grinding stone that was operated by turning a wheel. Nookie's stated that among his first creations were the S-hook and the hoe-wedge. Doyle's blacksmith shop did work for sugar cane field laborers. "Boss Doyle" and his apprentices sharpened hooks and the hoe-wedge. At the age of fourteen, Nookie made his own horseshoe and shod his own horse.

Rudolph "Boss" Doyle was trained as a farrier during the Danish period, so he knew how to care and treat horses, mules, and donkeys. He also knew about bush medicine and practiced it on animals. "Boss Doyle" used bush and rum to treat horses. Nookie learned about caring for horses from his father and even had a few racehorses of his own."

Will Thurland went to Nookie Doyle's blacksmith shop with his father Peter when they needed to get things done. "Nookie made the 'L' brackets for the lards that were on the mahogany bed frames. He used a one-inch piece of iron strip that he would heat, shape and bend into an 'L' shape so it would hold the mattress. Nookie also brazed, or joined together, the bandsaw for our cabinet shop when it broke. He used to solder the two metals together putting silver into the fire until it was red hot and apply it to the bandsaw. Then he would squeeze it to melt the silver and fuse the bandsaw together."

Sports writer Cherra Heyliger, in a 1990 racing program, wrote that Nookie, besides being willing to shoe horses, could observe what was wrong with a horse as it was moved about or cantered. "The problem Doyle believes with the injuries to horses nowadays is the constant track work, which hackles the animals." Doyle pointed out that the Danes and

8. Hugo "Nookie" Doyle Pounding Iron on His Anvil
Courtesy of Richard Schrader Sr.

the British used long road walks during the early morning to condition their horses and occasionally took the animals to the track.

Heyliger wrote that Nookie attended many horse races across St. Croix. He went to races at Jerusalem, the old Mannings Bay track, Betty's Hope, and even at Sugar Estate in St. Thomas. Nookie Doyle trained thoroughbreds and non-thoroughbreds at a few of the racetracks on St. Croix. Nookie trained the outstanding horse Bobby Sox for Christian Hendricks, which beat top horses like Beau Geste, St. Patrick, and Special Delivery. Doyle was involved in preparing Mademoiselle, Doughboy, Bobby Lang, Don Q, and Yankee Moon for race day. He told Cherra Heyliger that the greatest horses on St. Croix were Bobby Sox, Beau Geste, First Lord, Johnny Ace, Eagle, Lady Alden and Sir Thomas Moore. Nookie was familiar with horses such as Mariscal, Condado, Brass King and Lord Ruler that were owned by the Armstrong brothers. Nookie also was around Eastbourne, Wildfire and lots of other horses for Mr. Messer. Doyle was quoted saying, "There is an art and a science to the fitting of racing shoes, and if those shoes are not properly set, the best horses could be beaten by inferior horses."

Nookie, at the age of 23, took over the blacksmith shop at Bassin Triangle after the death of his father. He kept the tradition of training apprentices in his shop and also taught them about the care of horses. Nookie told Cherra Heyliger, "I never hide anything I know from the younger guys. What I learned from my father and others, I pass on to the younger generation. Long ago we used garlic, aloes, sulphur, ginger, oil of tar, and many other things which they do not use today, but the horses performed well."

Johannes "Junie" Lenhardt, from Christiansted, started as an apprentice to Nookie Doyle when he was 17 years old and helped out in the blacksmith's shop until Nookie passed away. "I lived six houses up the Peter's Farm hill from Nookie and would go after work and stay until eleven or twelve o'clock at night. Nookie learned the trade from his father and taught the same techniques to me. His father Rudolph Doyle and Joseph Foy, known as Master Wow, were located at the Bassin Triangle corner in Contentment. Doyle was by the former Legislature Building, and Master Wow was on the opposite corner.

As an apprentice, I used to blow the torch and fling the hammer. We made horseshoes and those were the easiest things to make. Together, we repaired the axels for horse and carts, and we shoed many horses for people. We made staples for the middle of wooden doors. When Nookie got a welding machine, we welded gates and mufflers for people."

Lenhardt reminisced, "Nookie used to bite his pipe while he worked. He would shout, "Humph, humph," when he knocked the hot iron. The apprentices I remember were Mambo, a jockey, and Tony Walters. Nookie had many customers who came by the shop, such as Leroy Henry, Duval Briscoe (the auto mechanics teacher at the Christiansted High School), and Mr. King, who lived across from Nookie. We made springs and other ironworks and parts for Mr. Clarence "Goosy" Harvey, who had trucks, and we even did an upright for one of the trucks."

Junie Lenhardt lamented not being able to secure any item from Nookie's shop as a keepsake. "I was unable to get anything from Nookie's shop after his death. I went back to the blacksmith shop up on Peter's Farm hill just two weeks after Nookie's death to look for the anvil, but the boys had sold it for little or nothing. Imagine, all of Nookie's tools were gone."

Gilbert Hendricks, a musician with Stanley and the Ten Sleepless Knights, was not an apprentice but spent many hours in the blacksmith shop with Nookie. It was Gilbert's love for horses that attracted him to the blacksmith shop. "Nookie was a mentor to me, and he helped me train horses because he liked how I used to talk about horses and the interest I showed in horse racing. Together we made horseshoes and a home brew of bagasse. He had a still that was used to make the bagasse for the horse rub and a little mixture for drinking. In his later years Nookie gave me that still and told me not to tell Duval Briscoe or Anselmo "Galento" Codrington, a horse trainer for Briscoe. Nookie believed in rubbing horses and using natural stuff not injections. For example, he made an oil rum to rub the horses' shoulders.

Nookie made horseshoes out of a flat iron that he bought from CUTCO, the Christiansted Utilities Corporation's store, which was located down on Strand Street in Christiansted. He would heat the iron until it got red and then pound it on the anvil. He would heat, bend, pound and pound. When he got the shape of the horseshoe, he would then drill holes into that piece of iron."

Doyle demonstrated his blacksmith techniques at the Annual Caribbean Folk Arts Festival, from 1984 to 1986, at the Island Center for the Performing Arts on St. Croix. Those summer shows were sponsored by the National Endowment for the Arts and the Virgin Islands Council on the Arts.

9. Hugo "Nookie" Doyle Shoeing a Horse
Courtesy of Richard Schrader Sr.

In 1990, Doyle traveled with the Virgin Islands participants to Washington, D.C. to showcase the islands' culture and traditions at the Smithsonian Folk Life Festival on the National Mall. He has been featured in several newspaper articles and documentaries on Virgin Islands craftsmen.

Hugo "Nookie" Doyle died at the age of 77 on June 22, 2000, at his residence. He was interred at the Christiansted Cemetery. The iron hinges that he made can still be found on windows and doors of buildings in Christiansted. Those items have stood up to the test of time and remain a testament to his skill as a blacksmith.

The Whim Museum has his pipe and several pictures on display that were featured in the 2014 Come Home to St. Croix exhibit called "Hass, Hassman, and Hass Racing." Horsemen remember Nookie, who put shoes on the majority of the horses for the races that were held thoughout the years on St. Croix.

Other notable St. Croix blacksmiths were Rudolph Doyle, Joseph Foy and Abraham Seeley from Christiansted, Christian Naughton and Alfred Lewis from Grove Place, and Dennis Boynes and Lazarus "Ballito" Halls of Lower Bethlehem.

ALFONSO S. FORBES
MASTER SHOEMAKER

Alfonso Sebastian Forbes was a master shoemaker and an excellent bandmaster on St. Croix during the early to mid-years of the twentieth century. He was a member of the Christiansted Industrial Brass Band and among the selected few from that Christiansted band that served in the U.S. Navy Band under the leadership of Alton Adams. Forbes would later organize a community band, which played in military parades and gave free musical concerts in Christiansted and Frederiksted playing military and popular tunes.

The *St. Croix Landmarks Society Research Library Notes* states, "Alfonso Forbes was born on December 24, 1895, in Christiansted to Richard and Clara Ebbesen Forbes. He attended the Danish Grammar School on King Street in Christiansted, which is today the Florence Williams Public Library. At the young age of eight he was apprenticed in shoemaking under the supervision of his father Richard and a relative, "Boss" Phaire. At the age of 16, Alfonso started his own shoemaking business and opened a shop on Company Street in Christiansted. At his shop, he made shoes for Danish soldiers and the local population."

Shoemakers, also known as cobblers, make and repair shoes, handbags and other leather items. Forbes would measure the person's feet and cut out the upper leathers for both feet according to the required size. These parts were fitted and sewn together on a stitching machine with a thick thread. The sole was then assembled, consisting of a pair of inner soles of soft leather, a pair of outer soles of firmer texture, a pair of welts or bands of flexible leather and lifts and top-pieces for the heels. The insole was attached to a wooden last, which was used to form the shoe. The lasting procedure secured the leather upper to the sole with tacks. The soles were hammered into shape; the heel lifts were then attached with wooden pegs. The finishing procedure consisted of smoothing, blacking, and burnishing the edges of soles and heels, and removing the lasts.

The tools Forbes used were mallets, awls (pointed tools for making holes in leather), and pegs or nails to fasten the shoes. He had three machines: a sewing machine, a stitching machine and a third machine. The cowhide, velvet fabric and the soles and heels were most likely imported from off island, primarily England. Buffing cloths for shining the shoes, as well as shoe polish, would be found in his shop.

10. Alphonso Forbes
Courtesy of the Forbes Family

Mrs. Rita Forbes, Alfonso's wife, gave two pairs of shoes that Al (Alphonso) had made for her to the Estate Whim Museum. One pair was a dark velvet dress sandal, and the other pair was made with leather. The items at the museum also include a velvet top hat that Al made for visits to Government House. Mrs. Forbes explained, "During the Danish times when men were invited to a function at Government House, they dressed in suits with tails and wore top hats."

11. Shoes Made by Alphonso Forbes
Two pairs of shoes, one velvet and the other leather, made by Alphonso Forbes for his wife Rita La Fontaine Forbes. Photo by Karen C. Thurland

In his spare time, Forbes became a member of Samuel "Sammy" Smith's band, the Christiansted Industrial Brass Band. On March 31, 1917, at the transfer ceremonies in Christiansted, Alfonso played his trumpet with the band at the lowering of the Danish flag and the raising of the American flag at Fort Christiansvaern.

On June 12, 1917, Alfonso Forbes enlisted as a musician in the United States Navy Band and served for four years. He joined as a "Second Musician" and was promoted to "First Musician." Mrs. Rita Forbes tells the story about the shoes Al made for Captain William Russell White, the commanding officer for the all-Black Navy Band that was stationed in St. Thomas. "Captain White was always limping, and one day Forbes inquired as to why he was limping. The captain said, 'Oh, my feet hurt with these shoes.' Al told the captain that he was a master shoemaker and could make him a pair of shoes. Captain White ordered the leather, and Al measured his feet and made him a pair of shoes. The captain tried on the shoes and said, 'These are the best shoes I have ever had.' Captain White was so pleased that he had Al make shoes for him and the other officers and later worked to get Forbes moved up in rank."

Ogese McKay, in his book *Now It Can Be Told*, wrote that Forbes also made shoes for the bandsmen. The men from the St. Croix bands were Alpheus Adams, Arnold Bolling, Redwood Davis, Alfonso Forbes, Anton Heywood, Vincent Jacobs, Paul E. Joseph, Ogese McKay, Eric Nielsen, Jacob Paulus, Alfred Simmonds, Wesley Thomas, Charles Thompson, Valdemar Thompson, Peter G. Thurland, and Theovald Wilson.

During his free time in the Navy Band, Forbes completed the required course of study by mail for the Vander Cook School of Directing and on January 18, 1919, received his diploma. Ogese McKay wrote that when Forbes showed the diploma to Mrs. White, the commanding officer's wife who was very influential in matters of the band, she said, "Forbes, you should be promoted at once." So Captain White instructed bandleader Alton Adams to change the rating of Forbes from Second Musician to First Musician.

While a member of the Navy Band, Forbes married Mary Eliza Krause on September 4, 1918. In 1921, after serving four years in the U.S. Navy, Forbes received an honorable discharge. Forbes was asked to re-enlist so he could go to Guantanamo Bay, Cuba with the Navy Band under the command of Alton Adams. But he said, "No, I am going to remain on St. Croix."

Throughout the years, Forbes maintained his interest in music and started a community musical band, where he served as conductor and bandmaster. He became known as the "March King" because of the military marches the band played marching down the streets of Christiansted and Frederiksted. In 1946, Forbes' band played in the funeral procession for Judge David Hamilton Jackson. The *Landmarks Research Library Notes* states that Forbes taught music to students at the Christiansted High School, the Claude O. Markoe Jr. High School, and in later years, the Pearl B. Larsen Elementary School. He also tutored private pupils and played taps with his trumpet at funerals for veterans.

12. Alphonso Forbes, the "March King."

Alphonso Forbes with his baton leading his band down King Street in Christiansted, St. Croix. The building on the right is Alexander's Gas Station and Insurance Office located on the corner of King Street and Smith Street. Courtesy of the Forbes Family

13. Alphonso Forbes with His Bugle Corps

Alphonso Forbes, far left, with his Bugle Corps playing for a military parade on King Street in Frederiksted, St. Croix. Axel Ovesen's Photo Shop is on the left. Courtesy of the Forbes Family

The *Landmarks Library Biographical Notes* states that Forbes, after his military days, resumed his shoemaking trade while pursuing a career as a bookkeeper. It further states that Forbes worked as a bookkeeper for local establishments such as Merwin's Hardware Store, John Alexander's, the Virgin Islands Corporation (VICORP), and the Arundel Corporation in St. Thomas. Mrs. Rita Forbes stated, "Al loved mathematics and was very good at it."

In the 1920s, according to the *Landmarks Research Library Notes*, when Ford cars were first brought to St. Croix, Forbes owned three cars and, seeing an economic opportunity, ran a taxi service between Christiansted and Frederiksted.

The *Landmarks Research Library Notes* states, "In September 1934, Forbes was issued a Burgher Brief as a merchant on St. Croix. He operated several businesses including two ice cream parlors, a boarding house at 59 Queen Street in Christiansted, which had a recreation center in the yard where he sometimes promoted boxing matches."

Berthill McGregor, the author's great uncle, fought several matches with the nickname "Kid Chocolate" in that yard. He was trained by James "Fine Works" Meyers, who was a policeman and also a mason. According to McGregor, those boxing matches cost $4.00 and were held on Friday nights. Leonard Larsen, who used to box in New York, was the referee. This yard was later used for a restaurant called Jose's Garden operated by the Marrero family.

14. The Former Forbes Boarding House
at No. 59 Queen Street in Christiansted.
Photo by Arol Abel

Forbes, being a military veteran, was among the group of veterans who started the first American Legion Post in the Virgin Islands, and he later served as the post commander. The American Legion Post No. 85 in Christiansted received its charter on February 11, 1942. The Post was originally named for Alexander Hamilton, the first Secretary of the United States Treasury, who lived and worked on St. Croix before he left to attend college on the mainland. Forbes was a member of the Selective Service Board for 15 years and also served as its chairman for several years.

After acquiring an interest in real estate, the *Landmarks Research Library Notes* reveals that Forbes bought and sold property around the island. One of his real estate deals was the sale of the original building to the Comanche Club owners. During those years, Forbes was frequently consulted as an appraiser of properties.

Mrs. Rita Forbes stated, "He had purchased the Comanche building from Joseph Alexander, a dry goods merchant and councilman. Al Forbes along with a Mr. Bough wanted to purchase the building on King Street in Christiansted where Alexander Hamilton worked as a youth, but Joseph Alexander sold it to someone else."

In 1947, Forbes began working at the Department of Public Works as a bookkeeper in the office on Hospital Street in Christiansted where the Virgin Islands Government offices were located across from the Old Danish Barracks. The Barracks building later housed the Department of Public Safety and the Department of Education. Alfonso Forbes worked for the territorial government for 25 years, and at the age of 77 retired from the Department of Public Works after 12 years of service in that department as a bookkeeper.

Alfonso Forbes was elected to the St. Croix Municipal Council (today the unicameral Legislature of the Virgin Islands) and served as secretary during his 1948-1949 term of office. His name is listed on a plaque in Government House in Christiansted.

In September 1949, Forbes married Rita Ramona La Fontaine from St. Thomas. Rita had lived in Puerto Rico and St. Thomas, where she attended Saints Peter and Paul Catholic School. Rita attended Girl's High School in Brooklyn, New York and went on to Pratt Institute for a year on a scholarship. She was accepted to the Julliard School of Music, where she studied for two and a half years. Rita

Forbes was a member of the Black Opera and did concerts in Puerto Rico, Jamaica, Cuba and Florida.

Describing her husband sewing skills, Rita said, "Al could sew, period. I had a lame' dress from New York and had some extra material. He made a men's tie to match my dress. He turned up hems on my dresses and took up the hems on his pants. When the collar for a shirt was worn out, Al would cut out the collar and turn the good part on the outside and sew it back onto the shirt. He did that for several of his friends."

Forbes had been offered a work scholarship at the leather shop at the Pratt Institute in New York. He turned it down stating that he preferred to remain on St. Croix.

According to the *Landmarks Research Library Notes*, Forbes, in 1953, was appointed warden at the Richmond Penitentiary, where he worked for three years with distinction. He received letters of commendation from insular Governor Morris F. de Castro and Rear Admiral A. K. Doyle.

In 1967 and 1968, as noted in the *Landmarks Research Library Notes*, Forbes earned 10 credits in psychology from the College of the Virgin Islands, St. Croix campus. During this time, Forbes and his wife Rita made guava jelly, which was sold at Rasmussen's Supermarket on Church Street in Christiansted, and they even sold it to businesses in Puerto Rico.

Mrs. Rita Forbes stated that when Al went to Denmark, he visited Queen Margrethe at her palace in Copenhagen. His friends asked him how he did it, and he said that he asked someone what he had to do to see the queen and was told to write his name on a piece of paper. So he put his name down and was selected to visit the queen and tour the Amalienborg Palace. He talked about making shoes in Danish times as he walked through the palace. Forbes, for a second time, along with his wife Rita met the Danish queen when she visited Government House in Christiansted in 1976, and they were invited to a reception by Governor Cyril E. King and Mrs. Agnes King.

As stated in the *Landmarks Research Library Notes*, Forbes, in his leisure time, besides being a musician, was an artist painting landscapes and creating woodcarvings. He served as the president of the St. Croix Art Guild, whose main goal was to promote local artists. Forbes was elected to life membership in the Virgin Islands Academy of Arts and Letters. He won an "Award of Merit" in 1971, by actively participating in the White House Conference Senior Portrait Cover Contest.

The *Landmarks Research Library Notes* further noted that Forbes, along with his wife Rita, was a member of the St. Croix Orchid Society. He was a charter member of the Rotary Club in Christiansted. Along with other Rotary members, Forbes participated in many conventions held in the United States and around the world including Mexico, Europe, and Australia.

Mrs. Forbes shared fond memories of her husband during our conversation. She said, "Al was a great guy and was very kind to me. After the doctor told me that he did not have long to live, I went to his bedside, and he told me to look in his shaving kit. When I opened it, I saw that he had an anniversary present for me. I found a beautiful diamond bracelet that Al had planned to give me for our anniversary. Even though he was sick, Al did not forget that important date."

15. Alphonso Forbes and His Band
Courtesy of the Forbes Family

Alfonso Sebastian Forbes died on August 21, 1976, at his home in Estate Altona. Left to cherish his life and accomplishments are his wife Rita La Fontaine Forbes and his two daughters, Juanita Forbes Gardine (deceased), who the public elementary school in Christiansted is named after and Liane Forbes-Fischer, school librarian at Pearl B. Larsen School. Alfonso had one son, Robert Alfonso Forbes, a former school teacher and career military man.

Other notable shoemakers were John Horton, Luther Thompson, and Christian "Pappy" Derricks from the town of Christiansted. Today men involved in the shoe trade are primarily engaged in shoe repair since shoes are mass produced in factories.

CARLOS H. MCGREGOR
TAILOR

C arlos McGregor learned the tailor trade from his father. He measured and made suits, shirts, pants, uniforms, and Bermuda shorts for his customers for many years. His leisure time was spent with the Christiansted Cricket Club (CCC) with whom he traveled to other Caribbean islands to compete in tournaments. Carlos McGregor was my maternal great uncle who showed me how to take up the hems for my brothers' school pants and to do button holes on shirts.

Carlos Heraldo McGregor was born on January 15,1902, in Christiansted, St. Croix to Charles Robert and Marie Gibbs McGregor. His father Charles was a master tailor, and his mother Marie was a seamstress. Mrs. Marie McGregor, affectionately called Doña Maria by Puerto Rican residents, used to tell her family that she was one of the first Puerto Ricans who came to St. Croix to live back in the late 1800's.

Carlos went to St. Mary's Catholic School, which was located on Prince Street in Christiansted where the convent was and is today, the Father Bradley Mission Center. He recalled that his first day was also the first day that the school opened at that site because it had been moved from Mount St. Mary's on Fisher Street and was brought down to Prince Street. Miss Alice Paulsen was the head teacher, and Miss Katie Visey was the other teacher. In those days the students had Book One, Book Two, and Book Three, and they read about Baby and Ann. The Belgian priests were in charge of the school, and the Belgian nuns came at a later time to teach.

Carlos stated, "My childhood friends were Joe Benjamin, Molke (Police Molke's son), and Van Brickman, and we played many games together. We used to play marbles, and I remember there was a game called 'hold beg.' That is, they would hit your knuckles with the marble and that used to hurt.

We played with a top made of wood called a tee-toe-top, which had a mark on each side. We made those tops ourselves. A top would have the letter A which stands for All, H for Half, N for None, and P for Put. You had to spin the top, and when it falls, the letter shows up. If it stops on A, all the thing that going around is yours; for example, if you are playing for money, all the money is yours.

16. A Tee-Toe-Top Made by Cyril Murphy
Photo by Karen C. Thurland

We used to fly kites. The first kite the children 'mek' we called a 'backee.' And that was what they used to write thing on. They take the strip from the cane peel and make a cross to put the paper on. And you had to put a tail on that to keep it down. Then you make a loop up to the top with a long string, and that string on the kite is to make it go up in the air and fly.

Then we went on to a bigger kite with wings on it. We made an American kite that had an American flag on it, or we would paint it red, white and blue with stripes on it. The Spanish kite had yellow and red colors, I think.

We played soccer football because the gendarme dem used to play that sport. I played soccer football at the Richmond School, which was a private school. The lady in charge of the school was Miss Hansen. They used to drive her across the street to what was called Aldersville. It had a lot of trees on both sides of that road where they would go right up and over the hill."

As was the tradition from years past during the early twentieth century, young boys had to learn a trade by becoming an apprentice with a master tradesman. Carlos McGregor studied under the watchful eye of his father Charles, who was a master tailor in Christiansted. Carlos McGregor said that he was a tailor, "All meh life," but at the time of the interview in 1982, he said that he had retired from working.

Carlos said that he had to learn the trade at his father's shop. He explained, "I would go to school half day, and the next half of the day I come home, and he would take me to the tailor shop, so I could learn the trade from him.

The tailor shop was located at No. 55 Company Street, and David Hamilton Jackson lived upstairs. Fredan owned it at the time."

My father (affectionately known as "Papa Mac" by his family and "Maestro Mac" by the general public) and all the fathers used to make it their business that their son takes the same trade as them. They teach their son whether their son likes that trade or not. You had to know your father's trade. In those days, children didn't have any say. Well, I didn't like the tailor trade so much, but I had to do it. What I did like was the carpenter trade and to be around the fellas. But my father used to tell me that the tailor trade is the best trade because you deh under shed all the time, and you ain't deh exposed to nothing else.

Papa Mac said, 'When you take a carpenter's trade, you deh all on house roof, and rain come and wet you down. All kind of things happen to you. It ain't a clean trade. The tailor trade is good.'"

According to Carlos, "You had to learn it even if you ain't like it because you are to tek in his footstep. So that is how I come by the tailor trade. The first thing he taught me was to make buttonholes and put on buttons. And next to surge out the seam them. Then afterwards, you were put on the machine, which you had to work with your feet on the pedal.

We used to have to pump the machine with our two feet. Sometimes we had to pump it all day till our feet hurt. The last machine we had was a Singer sewing machine, and nothing could beat that machine. When you work your feet, the wheel and the bobbin for the machine did the threading. That's how we did stitches.

As an apprentice, you start cutting out cloth and make lil' baby things like lil' pants for dolls and dressing the dolls. Then you moved up to making clothes for big people. There was a heavy scissor that we used to cut the cloth.

The cloth we used at the shop we got from local merchants, who sometimes got it from England. They had the best material for men's clothing and had the lining and everything. It seems like it was easier to get it from England. The Danish cloth used to be good, too. The merchants were old man de Chabert and Armstrong. They imported those goods for the island.

17. An Apprentice Learning the Tailor Trade
Photo by Alfred Paludan-Muller Courtesy of the Royal Library, Denmark

We used to make mostly dresses with a shaft and jackets with the high collar up to your neck. All the clothing was buttoned up to your neck, and they were mostly white.

And the poor people used to have that cloth that they call madras, a thicker cloth. And the men used to wear that with their pants. They had a thick shirt, not a jacket, just a thick shirt.

We worked mostly making uniforms for the police and all the officials like judges. There weren't too many tailor shops. We also made uniforms for the prisoners. There were only two tailor shops because most people used to do their own sewing in their own house.

There were lots of brass bands around in those days, and they had uniforms. Papa Mac used to make uniforms for them, too. He made uniforms for the Frank Cruse Band and for the Sammy Smith Band. Smith Band's house was in front of where our shop was, by the Limpricht Park, where the Calderon shop was located.

My father was gifted for making patterns. When we mek a suit, he put out a paper and then he punched holes round and round so that the paper only has punch holes in it. The person now comes and wants a suit of clothes, so Papa Mac will tek this paper and measure it and see if they agree with the measurement. Then, he knows this number paper pattern will suit you best, and he will mek the suit. He keeps the paper pattern for you special, and when you come back again, he ain't have no trouble. He just put it on the cloth and mark it around and mek a suit for you.

One day Mr. Victor Gibeon from Public Works came to the tailor shop and saw how my father made suits. So Gibeon told him, 'A person like you should have been in the States. You would have gotten a big job when they see what you do. They would put you in charge of designing all pattern works for people because they don't have that in the States.' But Papa Mac decided he ain't gon leave the island t'all. He said he ain't going nowhere.

The buttons we used were called 'bone' buttons. They were a hard button that used to come from away, and they came in all colors. You could get ah white one, ah brown one, and so forth. We got the buttons from Armstrong Store and Mr. Behagen Store.

We used a punch when we made a buttonhole. We cut the cloth and put it on the neck and then used the punch, which had a round head, to make a hole. Then we cut with a scissors. Finally, we knit the buttonhole with our hand going around and around with the needle and thread.

Our tailor shop was located across the market by the well, where Donald Abramson deh on King Street. Then we moved from there and came by the Pentheny Hotel, where Katy George had a house, and in front of her building was Lawyer Stakemann. The Lieutenant Governor's offices are located there today. Katy George used to work in his office.

They had a cotton ginnery where Brow Soda shop was later located. They used to mill the cotton. Cotton was grown at Estate Longford and at other places. Yes, we used to produce cotton on St. Croix. I remember a man named Solomon, who was sent to Denmark to learn the trade, and they gave him the different tools and sent him back to the island to work.

We stayed on King Street for a long time, and then we moved up to Gallows Bay to the Canegata property, the two-story building. Later we moved to Hamilton Jackson's place at No. 55 Company Street that was previously owned by Miss Furey.

I remember that Mr. Furey was a carpenter. Well, he used to mek coffins out of mahogany. He mek his own coffin, and he stored it in the upstairs of the house in the last building.

The sign my father had outside the shop on Company Street was made out of chalkboard with big letters. It read, 'Charles Robert C K McGregor, Master Tailor.'"

18. Carlos McGregor in His Workroom
Courtesy of Charles McGregor

Carlos McGregor stated that he witnessed the transfer of the island from the Danish to the American government. "I was 15 years old at the time of the Transfer, and I was living down on the wharf in that long row, today the King Christian Hotel. We had passed the 1916 gale in there. I went to listen because at that time I was in the tailor shop. I saw when the Marines come up in the truck, and they went up to the barracks. So I was inquisitive and went to see them. I could remember a couple of the first Marines that came here. There was this one fellow named Verdeber, Roderick's father, who was a Marine and was at the Transfer ceremony.

I wasn't sorry, and I wasn't glad to see the Danes go. I was glad to see the children take part in the ceremony. I was interested in the marching and everything. To me, the Danish gendarmes were the best in drilling. The U.S. Marines had a different way in drilling. The gendarmes were stiffer-like.

My family was undecided because they did not know what we were getting. They knew what we had, but they were not too anxious. But then again, the first and second year that the Marines were here we had a hard time with them.

The first set of Marines that came here came from Santo Domingo, and they had just come from ending a riot down there. They had that fighting spirit in them. So they used to go on bad in the night when they were on leave. They would come down in the town, and they start fighting with the people dem, and they had even shot a couple people.

And Hamilton Jackson at the time was the one that had to represent the people dem, and through that the Marines turned on him, and they threatened to shoot him. He had his office upstairs where the Savings Bank is now, and they fired shots up there at him, but they never did get him.

Then the Marines even started on the police dem. And the police got together and decided that they were not going to stand for the Marines beating up the people in town. So there was this one policeman by the name of Richardson, who was living down in Watergut at the time. He went after the Marines that was beating the people. He beat them up; he had them properly licked. The Marines decided that they were gon shoot him, and they were looking out for him.

He had to hide away, and his sister had lately come from the States, and she start to represent him. She went up in the barracks and complained to the captain, and she decided that if anything should happen to her brother they gon have to kill her too.

Policeman Richardson was taken aboard the mail boat and hidden in order to get him off the island. That's how he got away, and he never returned, not to my knowing.

And I remember when they were going to change the naval government to civil government. There was a meeting in the theater, and Hamilton Jackson, Doctor David C. Canegata and several other people was for the civil government. Ciple, the Cariso singer, got up and said, 'Well, we had a touch of the naval government, and I can't say what it will be like with the civil government, but at present the naval government is good to us.'

At that time they didn't have to pay for doctor, hospital or nothing. Anybody could ah go to the hospital and get free medicine. The Navy furnished all of that. There were the naval nurses here along with the native nurses whom they taught everything.

I remember one of the first naval nurses that came here was Mrs. Gibeon, but when she first came she was not married. Mr. Gibeon was an architect for the government, and he took sick, and through that he and she became quite friendly, and they got married.

Gibeon was one of the best architectural men here, and he got a job for me. He was the one who got a job for me at Public Works to go to the base (the airport). When work started on the base, I worked there from the beginning until they changed me and sent me up to East End. They had opened up a place there, and I was the first foreman that went up there to work with Neptune, the surveyor. He was a native and was the first surveyor to go up there and make a plan for the place.

All the laborers were from St. Croix, and even if they were from the islands they were living here for a long time. Workers were not imported from the islands for that job in East End.

Workers were imported to work in the cane fields, and the biggest bunch came from Barbados. They were mostly from Barbados, St. Kitts, Antigua and St. Vincent, but, you know, I have never heard of anyone from Trinidad coming here.

We had a coolie here back in the 1920s. He used to be watching up in the air and praying in his language. He used to be walking in the street and never used to have on any shirt. And he used to tek his two hands and say, 'Yo want to see me mek music. Give me a cent or two.' Then he clapped his two hands together and made a sound on both sides of his chest.

I remember Cornelius Pentheny had hired one they called Abdel. They had even named a horse after Abdel. Then we had one named Coolie Joe, who used to be in town and catch sprat. He was a sprat man, and he would be on the wharf just by the old library catching sprat there. Those coolies remained on St. Croix and died here. They did not go anywhere else.

Horse races were popular and were very good. My father Papa Mac had a horse by the name of Lord Salisbury. And he got that name from Dr. Canegata's father. He ran it under that name, and another time that horse ran under the name of Killer. He was a native, not an inbred horse. He used to beat all the other horses, and then they start bringing in horses to the island.

There was a man in Frederiksted who had a store up here in Christiansted that Miss Springer used to run for him. I believe that man's name was Mr. Calixte, and he had an English horse, but Lord Salisbury whipped him, too.

And then, Joe Bough had a horse they named De Foggy, and Salisbury beat him, too. They made a song out of it. They sang, 'Salisbury say, "Don't run De Foggy no more. There's a hot time in Cuba tonight.'

"I don't know why they sang about Cuba. I don't know if at the time Cuba been to war or not. That song was made up by people who used to go around singing Cariso, knocking the drum and thing. There was a woman who was a big Cariso singer, but I forgot her name. She used to go around in the foreday morning, and she always mek up these different songs.

Ciple, a Cariso singer, used to have a kerosene pan, knocking it and singing. I remember him singing, 'All the day they go say I gon to join the Union. Harness up the mule. Be careful how you whip.' He had liked to sing that song about the St. Croix Labor Union.

I was very active in sports. At the time the islands had belonged to the Danes, so they only used to play cricket and soccer football. We knew nothing about baseball in those days. Only a few people like the Armstrong dem that went to school up the islands played tennis.

I was always the first bat at the wicket. I used to longstop and sometimes played square leg. Those were the two positions that I played. I was on Dr. Canegata's team along with the three Armstrongs (Harry, Dicky and Douglas), J. Robert Smith and Bevy Anduze. We had a team of about 50 members when we started. The other supporting members were Bistrup, Hazlehurst, Steve Lantz, Harry Edwards and his father, and Emar Ramsey.

I bat bowl first to about fifth. My batting partner was Harry Edwards, and we always worked the wicket first because we used to go to break the bowling. We always gave a good show wherever we played, and the people used to praise us for our batting. Dr. Canegata played as wicket keeper, but he was the captain. And then afterwards, Douglas Armstrong took over as wicket keeper.

We practiced every day when we had the time. We practiced at Parade Ground (the D. C. Canegata Ball Park), and at that time I believe it belonged to Mr. Svitzer. Grove Place had a place to play where the park is now. Mr. Isaac Boynes was the captain for the Grove Place team, and he was also a member of the Municipal Council.

Almost every estate had a team. So when the Cup season come around, we had to travel from one estate to the next, and they used to come up to play our team. I was on the Christiansted team. There was a Grove Place team, a Mount Pleasant team, and Frederiksted had two teams. They had the Heroes and another team.

19. The Christiansted Cricket Club

The Christiansted Cricket Club (C.C.C.) were the winners of the 1929 Trophy. Front row: Left to right, Carlos McGregor, Bevy Anduze, and Harry Edwards. Second row: Left to right, Micah Rogiers, Harry Armstrong, Dr. David C. Canegata, Captain, Dicky Armstrong, Douglas Armstrong and J. Robert Smith. Third row: Both men are unknown.

Courtesy of the St. Croix Landmarks Society

The hardest team for us to beat was the Frederiksted team, the Frederiksted Cricket Club. The Christiansted team always come up at the top, and they would come out second. They have never won, at no time, a Cup match from us. We won the Cup for years.

We had another good team up here in Christiansted, the oldest team, called The Invincibles. James Martin was the captain of that team. Morris Davis had a team, but I forgot the name. And we had another team in Christiansted that was called the Chauffeur's Team, and that was a very good team, too.

We had another team, and that was an old team. The Danish Church parson had a team, but it was hard for them to play at Parade Ground, and they didn't have any other place to play. That is how they got that part of land, the Holger Danske. The parson gave the land that name, and his team was named the Holger Danske. And that name stayed even after the hotel was built down there.

We traveled for games, too. The first time the team traveled out was to go to St. Thomas, and our team was a young team with Dr. Canegata. Bistrup told us, 'Ayo going to meet those veterans over there like Mark Cruse, Baze, the Dove, Ralph Hendricks, and Brother Roberts. They are old and seasoned fellows. You all are a bunch of young fellows, you ain't gon get them out at all.'

So, with that in mind, we went, and what really happened was they whipped us, but we gave them a hard run. And afterwards, when we did go back to St. Thomas, we beat them. At that time, we had J. Robert Smith, who was pitching. We had Ross, Powell and Ejnar Bolling from Frederiksted.

Then we traveled to St. John. We went to Fish Bay and to Emmaus, and they were a very nice set of people that we met at the Moravian Church. Reverend Osborne was the parson there. The people lived just like one family, and they were all respectful and everything. We had a wonderful time over there. We also traveled to Tortola and St. Kitts. We didn't get to go to Antigua; Antigua came and played us.

We played cricket and soccer during the American time also, but they came in with baseball. The first people that started to play baseball along with the Americans were them boys in Gallows Bay. Most of those boys were hired to work around the Marines. People like Valdemar Rissing, Louis Stakeman and Charles 'Darkie' Thompson. They all tek up baseball. Maho James and his brother and all of them started baseball.

We always kept ourselves busy doing something or the other, and there were lots of sports like cricket, soccer football, horse racing, and swimming for young men."

McGregor, besides working as a tailor during the day, also worked as a night operator at the Telephone Exchange on King Street in Christiansted. He worked there with my aunt Genevieve "Jenny" Thurland for several years. In regards to the telephone system, which preceded the Virgin Islands Telephone Company, a student of mine at the then College of the Virgin Islands related a story to her fellow students and myself. Lurita King Boyd said, "I had called from New York City to leave a message for my mother and got Mr. McGregor on the phone. He immediately said, "Hold on; your mother just walked by the window. I will go and call her for you." The history class was amused hearing about communications in a small town where everyone practically knew everyone and how neighborly and considerate people were to each other.

20. Constable John Pearson and Carlos McGregor
Constable Pearson traveled from England to St. Croix to meet with
Carlos McGregor to get information about his Uncle Peter Carl
McKay, who was a racing tipster known as Ras Prince Monolulu
and was a famous Black man at racetracks throughout England.
Photo by Karen C. Thurland

Carlos Heraldo McGregor passed away from this life on March 11,1994, at his home in Old Hospital Grounds in Christiansted and was buried in the Christiansted Cemetery. Two and a half weeks later, his wife Elisa Lang McGregor followed him in death on March 29, 1994. He is survived by his sons Charles and Melvin McGregor, nine grandchildren and thirteen great-grandchildren and three great-great-grandchildren.

HALVER MOOLENAAR
MASON

The Thurland family has been acquainted with the Moolenaar family of St. Thomas for three generations. There are stories about that family and the mason trade in St. Thomas, so I added Halver Moolenaar, who lived on St. Croix, to my list of notable tradesmen. Growing up I heard about Uncle George, Aunt Cita (Terecita), Aunt Sule (Ursula Krigger), and the Jacobs family. I became acquainted with the majority of the family members when I visited St. Thomas or they came over to St. Croix.

The connection to the Moolenaars was further strengthened in 1976 when the new neighbors across from my parents' house turned out to be family of Halver's wife Jessica. They kept us informed as to the highlights of the Moolenaars on both islands.

Halver Leanzo Moolenaar was born on June 25, 1917, to Herman and Alberta Moolenaar at Estate Neltjeberg in St. Thomas. He attended the James Monroe Rural School for his elementary grades and completed his education at the Charlotte Amalie High School. He was sent to learn a trade with his uncle, George Moolenaar, who was a master stone mason on St. Thomas. Halver mastered the mason and construction skills and together with his Uncle George built many homes on St. Thomas.

Kathleen Rodgers in *Our Strummo* wrote about George Moolenaar. "George worked as a foreman at the Department of Public Works on St. Thomas from 1917 until 1954 when he retired as a master mason. He constructed and repaired many structures, which he planned and supervised during his time at Public Works. Among them are the Coast Guard Building, where he worked as assistant mason to John Bastian; the "finders" along the waterfront; the plastering of the 99 steps; Quarters B at Fort Christian; and the Senate Building. He also worked on the V. I. National Bank in Market Square and Hotel 1829. He also repaired the three cisterns at the Department of Education and supervised the construction and repair of schools such as James Madison, James Monroe and Jefferson."

George Moolenaar spoke to Ms. Rodgers about the construction of the Liberty Bell in Emancipation Garden, where his work of art is displayed in the base where different types of rocks are embedded and smoothed down to a nice finish. He considered the pillars located on top of Blackbeard's Castle as his masterpiece. The tools he used when doing construction were the trowel, which was known as the "dabbie," the plastering trowel, the cutting hammer, and the bull points.

Halver followed in his Uncle George's footsteps and entered the construction field. During the mid-1940's and up to the late 1950's, he was self-employed as a licensed general contractor. Halver was known for his exceptional block-laying skills. He worked on the construction of the Saints Peter and Paul Catholic School, the Virgin Islands Hilton Hotel, and the Charlotte Amalie High School.

Ingrid Hendricks Bermudez, Halver's stepdaughter, reminisced, "Halver came to St. Croix in March 1952, and was known in St. Thomas for laying 1,000 concrete blocks a day. He was recruited to work on the David Hamilton Jackson Terrace housing project because of his skill. His Moolenaar Construction Company was started in the late 1950s."

On St. Croix, Halver worked on the construction of the Alexander Hamilton Airport and numerous Federal Housing Administration (FHA) homes throughout the island. The Federal Housing Administration, legislated in 1934, provides mortgage insurance on loans made by FHA-approved lenders throughout the United States and its territories. The FHA insures mortgages on single family and multifamily homes including manufactured homes and hospitals.

Will Thurland, a joiner by profession, spoke about Moolenaar's masonry skills of laying hundreds of cement blocks a day and listed a few buildings he constructed. Mr. Thurland said, "Halver Moolenaar worked on the Charles H. Emanuel School, the Christiansted High School in Estate Richmond, and the Charles Harwood Hospital, also in Estate Richmond."

Marla Moolenaar, Halver's daughter, recalls that her father used to brag just about every day saying, "I laid 1,000 blocks a day. If I was doing that nowadays, I would be a millionaire." She said that he built several houses in Anna's Hope facing the Department of Public Works and worked on hotel construction. Marla fondly reminisced, "My father was a mathematician who knew measurement and spoke several languages."

James Sealey, former principal and district superintendent of schools, stated that Moolenaar built houses for both of his brothers and laid several hundred cement blocks in a day. Sealey explained, "Moolenaar had three pallets and two men helping him with the mortar and the laying of the blocks. Once you stretch a line you could move very fast and accurately."

Hubert Frederick worked as a foreman for Halver Moolenaar for five and a half years from the late 1950's to the mid-1960's. Fredericks stated, "We worked on FHA homes all over St. Croix, from Christiansted to Frederiksted, and even in La Vallee. We built houses for Mr. Roebuck in East End and for Kenneth Cooper across from the Richmond Post Office. I even worked on the Moolenaar family house in Estate Neltjeberg in St. Thomas and also did jobs on St. John."

Frederick learned construction from his father, who was a builder in Antigua. When Hubert came to St. Croix, he first did construction work with Ghirton Hector. Then, he did masonry and carpentry work for Halver Moolenaar. He explained that he worked head to head with Moolenaar and maybe that is why he was made a foreman. Moolenaar purchased the materials and supplies he needed from St. Croix Trading in Christiansted and from Clemente Cintron in Frederiksted.

Halver Moolenaar's funeral booklet gives us a glimpse of his work and leisure-time activities.

In 1970, Halver Moolenaar left the private construction sector and began a twelve-year career in the public sector with the Department of Education in charge of maintenance. He worked in this position until 1982, when he retired.

Halver, during his leisure time, concentrated on raising farm animals such as cattle, sheep and goats. He had a farm for his animals at Estate Bonne Esperance for several years.

He got involved in horse training and racing along with his friends Eric DeWindt and Raphael Millin. There was a big celebration in Estate Neltjeberg when his horse "Stardust" won a race.

Halver was a musician and proved to be an excellent guitar player. On visits to St. Thomas, he teamed up with his cousins, Colville and Lucien, and his aunt Terecita, who played the mandolin.

Halver, after moving to St. Croix, met and married Jessica Tutein from Gallows Bay. Jessica, a popular radio talk show personality, assisted Halver with his business. In 1954, she was the first Festival Queen for St. Croix.

21. Jessica and Halver Moolenaar
The Moolenaars after the March 31, 1967 Semi-Centennial Parade,
which celebrated the 50th Anniversary of the Transfer of the Danish
West Indies to the United States. Courtesy of Marla Moolenaar

Halver's daughter Magda wrote, in his funeral booklet, a few memories about her childhood days with her father. She recalled, "You would leave your weekend to do fun things – like going to Buck Island on a Sunday, or getting up real early on a Saturday and going to Annaly for mangoes. Or even better, going to St. Thomas to see our grandparents, sisters, brothers, and other family members. I even remember when you and Mommy would take a truckload or car load of children with us to the good ole drive-in theater."

Ingrid Hendricks Bermudez stated, "Halver's greatest joy after Hurricane Hugo of 1989 was speaking with the people he built homes for back in the 50s and 60s. They came to

22. The David Hamilton Jackson Terrace
Courtesy of the Virgin Islands Housing Authority

23. The Charles Harwood Memorial Hospital
Photo by Karen C. Thurland

his home looking for him to tell him that their house had withstood the hurricane winds."

Halver Moolenaar passed away on Sunday, October 5, 2003, and was interred in the Christiansted Cemetery. He will be remembered as a master mason, who laid hundreds of cement blocks in a day and constructed numerous houses throughout the Virgin Islands.

A few notable contractors from Christiansted were the Hector brothers (Ghirton, Winthrop, Herman and David), who built or renovated several houses in Christiansted and its outskirts. According to Delano King, his father Ezekiel King, a contractor, built houses on St. Croix including the Mrs. Elena Christian and Ejnar Bolling houses on King Street, the Judge Almeric Christian's building and Keith Forbes buildings on Company Street, the Steele and Grant houses in Estate La Grande Princesse, and the Messer house in Estate St. John. Delano worked with his father when he was a teenager.

Peter "Boss Pete" Jackson, from Watergut, was a carpenter and contractor, who built houses all over the island. Gloria Gibbs Bell remembered, "He did work on the addition to the Comanche Hotel in Christiansted and worked as a foreman overseeing the construction. He did work for the Armstrongs, the Flemings, and several other businessmen."

A few notable masons from Christiansted were Donald Pickard, Thomas Williams, Paul James and Alfredo Lawrence from Gallows Bay, and they are just a few of the tradesmen who contributed to the development of St. Croix. Hubert Frederick sums it up saying, "Today, masons do additional work such as carpentry and plumbing and are referred to as tradesmen."

PETER HORATIO THURLAND
GOLDSMITH

P eter Horatio Thurland was born Free in 1835 in Christiansted to Marie Johanne Cisco, a Free woman, and George Thurland, a goldsmith. His maternal grandmother was Bethsheba Christopher, who was also a Free woman. Bethsheba's parents were Christopher, an Amina African, and Naemi, a Watje from Africa.

Peter H. Thurland probably learned the goldsmith trade from his father George Thurland, who is listed in St. John's Anglican Church records from the 1780s. George Thurland is listed as white and in 1820 married Frances Owen, a Free Colored woman, whose father Charles Owen was also a goldsmith. Frances died in 1829, and George began a relationship with Marie Johanne Cisco in the early 1830's. George Thurland had two sons with Cisco, John George in 1832 and Peter Horatio Thurland in 1835. Peter H. Thurland along with his brother John George Thurland were confirmed in the Lord God of Sabaoth Lutheran Church on King Street in Christiansted. They were both listed as free born since their mother Marie was a Free woman.

The author and her family are descended from John George Thurland, who later dropped John from his name. In one or more of the census reports, he is listed as George Thurland Jr.

24. A George Thurland Silver Spoon
Photo by Anne Thurland

25. Karen Thurland Holding a George Thurland Silver Spoon
at the Danish National Museum. Photo by Anne Thurland

Danish Census records show Peter, George and their mother Marie living at No. 54B Berg Gade (Hill Street) in the Free Gut neighborhood in the 1841 population count. The two brothers and their younger sister Eugenia Clendenen were listed as students. In the 1850 Census, still living at the Hill Street residence, George at the age of 18 was listed as a goldsmith, and Peter at 15 years was an apprentice. By 1855 Peter, at 20 years old, was a goldsmith and owned the house on Hill Street along with Johannes Bowman, who was married to his mother Marie Cisco.

Peter Horatio Thurland moved to St. Thomas some time in 1860 and remained there for several years working as a goldsmith. That same year Peter had a son, Peter Carl Washington Thurland, with Adriane Dohnert, who remained on St. Croix. In the 1870 Census, Peter is listed as a goldsmith living at 53A Dronningens Gade (Queen Street) in Charlotte Amalia [Amalie] with a family that was originally from St. Croix and St. Eustatius.

The 1880 Census has Peter Thurland back on St. Croix and as the owner of the house at No. 54B Hill Street, living with his mother Maria Cisco Bowman. According to the 1890 Census, Peter lived with his wife Helen at No. 1 and 2 Hospital Street, which he owned. They lived at No. 1 Hospital Street according to the 1901 and the 1911 census reports.

Peter H. Thurland worked with the preparation of the Danish Census for 1911 and signed the pages to validate the people who lived on Hospital Street in Christiansted. He was one of the signers along with other prominent community

26. John George Thurland, a Christiansted Goldsmith, Born Free in 1832
Courtesy of Will Thurland

27. Peter Horatio Thurland in His Goldsmith Shop
The young man in the background is probably his son, Peter Carl Washington Thurland. Notice the shop's sign in the background.
Photo by Alfred Paludan-Muller Courtesy of the Royal Library, Denmark

members such as William Messer and Theodora Dunbavin of Watergut.

Peter H. Thurland spent time working for improvements in his community and was involved in several organizations. One such organization was the Committee of the Danish Temperance Society of the Blue Cross.

Both the *St. Croix Bulletin* and *The St. Croix Avis* newspapers carried the story of the opening of a coffee tavern or tea-house in Christiansted on January 4, 1900, by the Committee of the Danish Temperance Society of the Blue Cross. Rev. Hermann Lawaetz was the chairman, and the members were Cornelius Crowe, Sergeant Hansen, Peter Thurland, A. Schon, Charles C. Reubel and Samuel A. Smith. The papers quoted Rev. Lawaetz on the opening at the southwest corner of the market. Rev. Lawaetz explained that the Society had entered on the undertaking in order to supply at a cheap rate warm tea or coffee, and other non-alcoholic refreshments to all who needed them, and who otherwise might go to rum-shops. The Society had taken the work in hand because the members saw the need for it.

Peter Horatio died on February 8, 1913, at his home at No. 1 Hospital Street. David Hamilton Jackson, in the *St. Croix Avis* newspaper of February 15th, 1913, wrote about the passing and funeral of Peter Thurland.

ST. CROIX AVIS

Proklama.

ALLE og enhver, som maatte have noget at fordre i Boet efter afgangne Guldsmed PETER HORATIO THURLAND og efterlevende Enke, hvilket Bo behandles ved nærværende Skifteret, indkaldes herved med 3 Maaneders Varsel til at anmelde og bevisliggöre deres Krav.

Christiansteds Skifteret, St. Croix, den 13de Februar, 1913.

POULSEN.

Abonnement

paa Aviser og Blade maa tegnes inden Maanedens Udgang.

Christiansted Postkontor, den 14de Februar, 1913.

M. ANDERESN.

THE AVIS.

Christiansted, St. Croix.

Saturday, 15th February, 1913.

The s.s. "Parima" from New York via St. Thomas was expected to arrive at Frederiksted at 5 o'clock yesterday afternoon, sailing about noon to-day.

The s. s. *Guiana* for New York is due at Frederiksted Wednesday morning 6 o'clock, sailing soon after.

In the *Bulletin* of 27 January we published a telegram to the effect that M Van Biene, a composer of broken music, had died suddenly on the stage. What "broken music" was we did not know and could not find out. It now appears from an interesting article in the *New York Times* of 24 January, that the reference was to a composition entitled "The Broken Melody" of which Van Biene was the author.

The paragraph from *The Times* will be found below.

VAN BIENE, COMPOSER, DIES ON THE STAGE.

Noted 'Cellist, Author of "The Broken Melody," Expires in English Music Hall.

LONDON, Jan 23—Auguste Van Biene, known to theatrical audiences all over the world as the composer and player of "The Broken Melody," died on the stage of the Hippodrome at Brighton to-night.

The haunting refrain of "The Broken Melody" had inspired over 6,000 audiences before its composer brought its career to an end.

"If I had not done so," he once said, "it would have driven me to a lunatic asylum."

"The Master Musician" was its successor. For some time it was played in theatres, but recently a shortened version occupied a place in music hall programmes. Like "The Broken Melody," it afforded Van Biene an opportunity for some wonderful 'cello playing. Three solos were his share of the melody, and the last was "Home, Sweet Home." At the conclusion the curtain was rung down on the musician, collapsed in his chair.

Van Biene went through the act at both performances to-night. When he fell back in his chair at the second performance, nobody in the audience thought it more than the prescribed dramatic finish to the scene. The stage manager, however, noticed unaccustomed realism about it, and the curtain was rung down more hurriedly than usual. When the stage manager went to the actor, he found he was past human aid. Van Biene was dead when lifted from the chair.

Van Biene had a romantic career. He was born in Holland sixty-three years ago, and came to England early in life. When a boy of 17 he was discovered playing a 'cello in Hanover Square by Sir Michael Costa, who, remarking the boy's wonderful power... formances he collected money for the Music Hall Benevolent Fund.

The story of "The Broken Melody" was partly founded on the composer's early struggles, the haunting melody, which runs through the play, being composed on a train journey from Brighton to London.—*New York Times, 24th Jan.*

FELLOW CITIZENS PAY TRIBUTE TO THE LATE PETER THURLAND.

NATIVE BRASS BAND IN ATTENDANCE

BRAND MAJOR AND OFFICERS AT ATTENTION AS CORPSE ENTERS CHURCH.

BY D. HAMILTON JACKSON.

This paper has recently chronicled the death of a well known and faithful member of the Lutheran Mission Church, and a well-deserving tribute was there paid her by the pen of a friend. To-day it falls to me to recount, through these columns, to his friends far away the death of an esteemed citizen of our town, Mr. P. H. Thurland. If in the following delineation of character, I overdo justice, it is only because I am led away by my feelings:—Unassuming, yet dignified in dealing with his fellow men; honest in his dealings as a professional jeweller; reliable for a given word, and always ready to please—such were his qualities, unexaggerated.

The deceased was prominent in almost every calling here. He was a Warden of his church, a Freemason, an Odd Fellow, First officer of the Brand Corps, and some years ago was connected with the Cemetery Commission. He was even on the political platform, and was unanimously elected chairman of an electoral meeting some years ago.

The Obsequies.

Gathered at his home on Sunday afternoon (9th inst.) was a large concourse of friends, who had come to pay him their last respects. Looking around, one could at once see what kind of man was to be carried away from that house—enveloped in a beautiful sand-papered-coffin with silver mountings; carried upon a carriage-part drawn by his pet cream—to the last resting place of man—the grave.

As the procession neared the church, it was greeted by the Native Brass Band playing the Dead March (Webster's Funeral March), while six sergeants of the Fire Brigade received the corpse at the steps of the church, where also had gathered the Brand Major and officers of the Brigade and other gentlemen and ladies. It is a rare thing to have martial music at the funeral of a civilian to guide the steps of the followers, and on this occasion the Boys looked so neat in their white uniforms and played with all their might, that one could not help admiring them as they tried to do their best.

It was a long time waiting for the service to commence, as the gathering, being so large and the church being so small, it was difficult to find seats, and many had to remain outside. In the church the ceremony began with the singing of the hymn "Abide with me" after which the "Funeral Psalm" (90th) was read by the pastor Mr. Helweg-Larsen, who afterwards spoke from the text "To meet thy God, prepare oh Israel!" The congregation and choir then sang "Jesus lover of my Soul", which closed the services in the church. The procession formed again and marched off to the cemetery, headed by the Band playing the aforementioned march, where the ceremony of interment was performed, after which the Band played "Nearer my God to Thee" while the earth closed its door over the corpse.

Thus was laid to rest one of our most popular and respected citizens, who has left behind a sorrowing widow, to whom all who read this paper will, I hope, join in extending their heartfelt sympathy, and those upon whom the management of the affairs of the island rest, might show theirs in a more lasting and tangible form.

Christiansted, 10th Feb. 1913.

Dear Mr. Editor,

Somewhere in the Book of the Pro-... an end, for as I passed by yesterday morning, the pleasing sight of a man at work, making the weeds disappear, caught my eye, and on mentioning this to a friend I was informed that a bust of our late and much beloved Governor is shortly to be erected in the "garden",—an excellent idea.

Now that the "garden" is being cleaned, (and I'm sure, going to be kept clean) I would like to make a few suggestions, hoping the Embellishment Committee (if such a committee exists) or, at any rate the persons responsible for the cleaning, may see them, and give them their favourable consideration.

Besides cleaning the garden, I would suggest:

1. That the garden be furnished with a few decent-looking benches (not exactly like those on the wharf.)
2. That the present huge fence and gate be removed and a low iron rail be put in its stead, similar to that used by the Embellishment Committee of our sister island, St. Thomas, and then let the garden be open to the public, where (perhaps) our bands will play occasionally, and our children will be permitted to play under the shady trees.

If this could be realized, why, we would be obliged to rejoice and sing "this land that was desolate, is become like the garden of Eden".

With much thanks,

I am yours faithfully,

ADAM.

Christiansted, 12th Feb 1913.

PASSENGERS.

Christiansted.

Feb. 8th—Dannebrog from St. Thomas—Mr. & Mrs. Walleker and 2 children, Dr. Gordon, Miss Gordon and servant.

Feb. 12th—Vigilant from St. Thomas—F. Humphrey, C. Humphrey, B. Vanterpool, A. Benjamin, S. Jacobs, M. Huyghue.

Feb. 13th—Dannebrog for St. Thomas—O. H. Schmiegelow, Chr. Ettrup.

Feb. 13th—Vigilant for St. Thomas—Alberta Christian, Else Petersen, Alexander Marshall.

TELEGRAMS

ST. CROIX STATION.

London, Feb. 12th—The suffragettes have smashed the windows of the Carlton, Junior Carlton, Reform and Oxford and Cambridge Clubs, also of Schomberg House, the residence of Prince Christian. Several were arrested and declared themselves delighted.

Grace Branson, their leader, was sentenced to two months' imprisonment and others to ten days.

Mr. McKenna, the Home Secretary, has ordered an inquiry into Miss May Billinghurst's charge of brutality in connection with forcible feeding in Holloway Prison, where she was serving a sentence of eight months, but had to be discharged after one week, having become ill.

Mr. W. E. Guinness, M. P. for Bury St. Edmunds, testifying before the Marconi Investigation Committee, said that after hearing Mr. Lawson's evidence, he thought portions of the articles which he (Mr. Guinness) had published in the "Outlook," were ill advised, but he disclaimed any intention of making personal attacks upon Ministers.

Advices from Tokio state that the Premier appealed to the Mikado from the Diet's vote of want of confidence, and that a popular demonstration followed Prince Katsura's communication to the Diet of the Royal support of the Liberal Party. The Opposition acquiesced, but the Diet ignored it. The populace later stoned the Premier and attacked the office of a newspaper supporting him, and fought the police with the result that several were killed and scores wounded.

The Diet has adjourned for three days.

It is announced that the Kaiser's daughter Princess Victoria Louise, is betrothed to Prince Ernest, the Duke of Cumberland's son and heir, thus removing the last obstacle to the unity of Germany. The couple first met at Potsdam in June last.

The Turks report that the Adrianople gar-

28. The *St. Croix Avis* Article
About the Funeral of Peter H. Thurland. Fair Use

Today it falls to me to remember through these columns, to his friends far away the death of an esteemed citizen of our town, Mr. P. H. Thurland. If in the following delineation of character, I overdo justice, it is only because I am led away by my feelings – Unassuming yet dignified in dealing with his fellow men; honest in his dealings as a professional jeweler; reliable for a given word, and always ready to please – such were his qualities, unexaggerated.

The deceased was prominent in almost every calling here. He was a Warden of his church, a Free Mason, an Odd Fellow, First Officer of the Brand Corps, and some years ago was connected with the Cemetery Commission. He was even on the political platform, and was unanimously elected as chairman of an electoral meeting some years ago.

Jackson wrote of the gathering at the house at No. 1 Hospital Street, how Mr. Thurland was laid out, the procession to the church, the service and the interment:

Gathered at his home was a large concourse of friends, who had come to pay him their last respects. Looking around, one could at once see what kind of man was to be carried away from that house – enveloped in a beautiful sandpapered-coffin with silver mountings; carried upon a carriage.

As the procession neared the church, it was greeted by the Native Brass Band playing the Dead March (Webster's Funeral March), while six sergeants of the Fire Brigade received the corpse at the steps of the church, where also had gathered the Brand Major and officers of the Brigade and other gentlemen and ladies. It is a rare thing to have martial music at the funeral of a civilian to guide the steps of the followers, and on this occasion the boys looked so neat in their white uniforms and played with all their might, that one could not help admiring them as they tried to do their best.

It was a long time waiting for the service to commence, as the gathering, being so large and the church being so small, it was difficult to find seats, and many had to remain outside. In the church the ceremony began with the singing of the hymn "Abide with Me" after which the "Funeral Psalm 90th" was read by the pastor Mr. Helweg-Larsen, who afterwards spoke from the text "To Meet Thy God, Prepare Oh Israel!" The congregation and choir then sang "Jesus, Lover of My Soul," which closed the services in the church. The procession formed again and marched off to the cemetery, headed by the Band playing the aforementioned march, where the ceremony of internment was performed, after which the

Band played "Nearer my God to Thee" while the earth closed its door over the corpse.

Thus was laid to rest one of our most popular and respected citizens, who has left behind a sorrowing widow, to whom all who read this paper will, I hope, join in extending their heartfelt sympathy, and those upon whom the management of the affairs of the island rest, might show theirs in a more lasting and tangible form.

29. A Gold Ring Made by a Thurland Goldsmith
Photo by Karen C. Thurland

30. A Thurland Ring and a Goldsmith Anvil
Photo by Karen C. Thurland

Peter H. Thurland's house at No. 1 Hospital Street had a few owners after his death and was even used as a junior high school after the 1928 gale (hurricane). His great-nephew Peter Gregory Thurland purchased and renovated that house several years later and operated a cabinet shop on the bottom floor. The family members, unfortunately, have none of Peter H. Thurland's jewelry. All they have is a small anvil that he used when conducting his trade.

The author was fortunate to acquire an image of Peter H. Thurland from the Danish Royal Library's digitized collection on the Internet. Anne Walbom, a member of the Danish West Indian Society, had informed me of the image and emailed the information regarding who to contact to get permission to use the image in this book. The news article on Peter H. Thurland, which gave valuable information, was obtained from the research library at the Whim Plantation Museum.

PETER G. THURLAND SR.
MASTER CABINETMAKER

P eter Gregory Thurland was born on February 19, 1892, in Christiansted, Danish West Indies. His parents were George Thurland, a jeweler, and Sarah Bryan. Peter descended from a long line of Free men who were goldsmiths and silversmiths. The Thurlands, according to baptism and marriage records of the St. John's Anglican Church and the Friedenstahl Moravian Church have lived on St. Croix since the late 1700s.

Peter was raised by his godparents, Henry and Anna Thomas, who belonged to the Catholic church. Therefore, Peter was baptized at Holy Cross Catholic Church, and he attended Mount St. Mary's School, a Roman Catholic school, located on the hill above Christiansted adjacent to Fisher Street. The lay teachers, Miss Vicky and Miss Kassis, taught reading, arithmetic, history, and writing. Religious instruction was an important part of the curriculum. Peter studied Book One, Book Two and up to Book Six and even learned trigonometry in his last year at school. Peter loved to play music and read books. He spent most of his leisure time practicing on his instrument or reading any book he could get his hands on.

At the young age of eight, Peter learned woodworking when he was apprenticed to the joiner shop of Peder

Pedersen. Pedersen, a strict disciplinarian, greatly influenced his young apprentice. Peter continued with woodworking for several years, even though his father asked him to work in the family jewelry shop. Peter refused his father's offer because he wanted to become a cabinetmaker and make fine furniture.

After completing his studies at Mount St. Mary's School, Peter worked for a short time at the cotton ginnery at Estate Constitution Hill. He said, "I was fascinated with machines. Although the field workers made more money, I worked inside the ginnery where we used the machines."

At the age of 14, Peter went to work at the Bethlehem Sugar Factory, which was the heart of the island's agricultural economy. Peter earned fifty cents a day doing carpentry work and even carried his own tools to work. At various times he was sent out to different estates to work on the great houses. He designed the spiral stairs for the Bonne Esperance Great House. Peter excelled in his work and soon became a foreman with a crew to supervise. One of the projects Peter and his crew worked on was the renovations for Peter's Farm Hospital near the Christiansted Cemetery after the 1916 gale caused considerable damage to that facility.

At the turn of the century, native brass bands provided monthly musical concerts throughout the island. One such band was the Christiansted Brass Band organized by Clifford Adams in 1908, and that band played on the Christiansted wharf on Sunday afternoons. Peter played a tenor horn in the Christiansted Brass Band, under the leadership of Frank Cruse, and was tutored by Svend Svendsen, a Danish musician. The instruments the band used were the property of the Brand Corps (Fire Department) for whom the band played at monthly fire drills.

Several members of Cruse's band later joined the Christiansted Industrial Brass Band directed by Samuel A. Smith, the principal of the Christiansted High School. Peter played a slide trombone in this band. The band played at concerts, in parades, and for government functions, such as the twenty-fifth wedding anniversary of Governor Helweg-Larsen. Contributions for band instruments were made by prominent citizens. The band's uniforms were made by Charles R. McGregor, a master tailor in Christiansted.

It was the Christiansted Industrial Brass Band that played the Danish National Anthem at the March 31, 1917, transfer ceremony in Christiansted. Peter played his trombone as the Danneborg, the Danish flag, came slowly down the flagpole at Fort Christiansvaern. This solemn occasion marked the transfer of the islands from Denmark to the United States of America.

Shortly after the transfer of the islands, the U.S. Government declared war on Germany, thus entering into World War I. Inhabitants of the islands did not become citizens until 1927, so the military draft did not include them. However, U. S. Navy Captain William Russell White recruited members for a military band to be stationed in the islands. Alton Adams, leader of Adams Juvenile Band of St. Thomas, was selected as the bandmaster. Captain White and Adams listened to selections rendered by the Christiansted Industrial Brass

31. The Christiansted Industrial Brass Band

The Brass Band with their flag marching to the Christiansted wharf to give a free Sunday afternoon concert. Notice the CIBB initials in the flag. Photo by Andreas Lauridsen   Courtesy of the St. Croix Landmarks Society

Band, the Christiansted Brass Band under Jacob Paulus, and the Frederiksted Brass Band under Eric Nielsen and chose the strongest players. Peter Thurland, an accomplished trombonist, was selected along with Alphonso Forbes, Redwood Davis, Jacob Paulus, Ogese McKay, Charles Thompson, Victor Thompson, Anton Heywood, Paul E. Joseph, Arnold Bolling, and Alfred Simmonds.

These men were enlisted in the United States Navy as second class musicians, receiving equal privileges and the same salaries as all other bands in the Navy. As a first class musician, Jacob Paulus received a pay rate of $56.00 per month while the other musicians received $50.00 monthly.

The newly recruited band members did regular routine duty for four years. The Navy Band was attached to the *U.S.S. Vixen* stationed in St. Thomas. However, the St. Croix contingent remained on their home island until all 22 members were recruited. These men built the bandstand on the Christiansted wharf when they were not on drills. Peter was happy to do carpentry work on the music pavilion, where the band gave concerts. In 1918, the St. Croix band members were ordered to St. Thomas for "special training" that Adams had requested for them.

Adams, a strict band leader, was especially hard on the Crucian musicians. Ogese McKay, a Navy Band member, recalled a particular incident with Adams. In an interview, McKay said, "We were unable to purchase the white military caps because Adams refused to give us the company's mailing address, so we could order our own caps. Peter Thurland, being the positive thinker that he was, got together with Alphonso Forbes and together they made their own white caps. Eventually, they made caps for all the St. Croix members. Those caps were almost identical to the Navy's military caps."

The St. Croix band members stayed in St. Thomas for approximately one year. After a command performance by the Crucians, Captain White determined that no more training was necessary. The Crucian members could play good music and were allowed to go back to St. Croix. Peter returned to St. Croix and played in the Christiansted contingent of the Navy Band. The band held monthly concerts and played in the Christiansted bandstand. Their musical selections included marches, overtures, and waltzes.

When the Navy decided to station the Navy Band at Guantanamo Bay, Cuba, Peter took the option of leaving the Navy. He received his honorable discharge as a first class musician on September 20, 1921, and with his discharge payment set out to open his first cabinet shop.

In addition to opening his own cabinet shop, Peter began teaching in 1921 at the Christiansted Public Grammar School on King Street (today the Florence Williams Public Library) where he taught manual training to boys in grades four through six. In an interview, Theodora Dunbavin, a noted educator, remarked, "Mr. Thurland had a good rapport with the boys and aided the teachers with discipline problems."

Later he taught manual arts, woodworking, and carpentry at the Christiansted High School. There he worked with fellow educators Claude O. Markoe, Elena Christian, Juanita Gardine, Alatha Williams, Edna Coff, Wilfred James,

Clarissa Jackson Creque, Darwin Creque, Ruth Heywood, Beryl Hansen, and Enid K. Hodge.

In 1932, Peter moved to the newly established St. Croix Vocational Institute, which was located in Estate Anna's Hope. The curriculum offered a wide range of subjects such as agronomy, agricultural engineering, farm mechanics, building construction, auto mechanics, shoe making, tailoring, general science, and the basic academic subjects. At that time the average teacher's salary was about $50.00 per month. Young men from St. Thomas came over to attend the vocational school. A few of Peter's students from St. Thomas were Alphonse LaBorde Sr., Titus Carrington, Hugo Malone, and Franklin Francis.

In 1941, Peter received a scholarship to attend the University of Puerto Rico at Rio Piedras. He enrolled in the summer session where he took vocational courses. Fellow educators Claude O. Markoe and Elena L. Christian also attended at the same time.

Alphonse LaBorde, a student from St. Thomas, fondly recalls Mr. Thurland's love for classical music and his ability to teach all the instruments. When the Institute closed in 1942, Peter returned to teach at the Christiansted High School in the old Barracks Yard on Hospital Street.

32. The Faculty of the Christiansted High School in 1944
Front row: Left to right, Mrs. Edna Coff, Miss Esther John, Mrs. Elena Christian, and Mrs. Alatha Williams. Second row: Left to right, Claude O. Markoe, Principal, Miss Beryl Hansen, Mrs. Clarissa Jackson Creque, Mrs. Enid K. Hodge, Miss Merle Christian, Mrs. Ada B. James, and Peter G. Thurland Sr. Courtesy of Will Thurland

Beginning in 1921, Peter rented space for his cabinet shop at various places throughout the town of Christiansted. His first workshop was located at No. 43 King Street near the corner of King and Prince Street. The second shop was at Robert Merwin's Lumber Yard at No. 38 Strand Street, today the Caravelle Arcade. The third shop was on the waterfront in the King Christian Hotel building until that shop was destroyed by the 1928 hurricane. Peter then moved his business to a long row building on Church Street. The fifth and final site for Thurland's Cabinet Shop was in the basement of a three-story house at No. 1 Hospital Street, which he purchased in 1931 from Carl Rohlsen. This building was originally owned by Peter's great uncle Peter Horatio Thurland, a noted jeweler.

Peter and his sons Will, Pete, and Albert cleaned the debris from the bottom floor on No. 1 Hospital Street so that the cabinet shop could be established there. After the renovation was completed, Peter sent purchase orders to the U.S. mainland for a table saw, a lathe, drill press, chisels, and a concave/convex plane. Peter made the regular wood planes himself. He obtained a band saw through his friend Joseph Leader, brother of Attorney Amphlett Leader, who worked at the Bethlehem Sugar Factory and knew that the managers had no more use for that piece of equipment.

33. Peter G. Thurland's First Mahogany Chair, Made in 1913
Photo by Karen C. Thurland

Peter repaired mahogany furniture and also began to make new furniture, trying different techniques and styles. Most of the styles were the Queen Anne, Chippendale, and Hepplewhite. He specialized in making chairs, tables, rocking chairs, planters' chairs, picture frames, coffins, caskets, jewelry boxes, trays, bowls, lampstands, bookends, and frames for wall mirrors. These he patterned from books he bought or borrowed from the library. At customers' requests, he made small mahogany chests according to their specifications. Many of his customers were Navy officers and estate managers.

Peter used native woods, such as mahogany, thibet, sandalwood, saman, mango and lignum vitae, to make his furniture and other items. Mahogany logs were obtained from the estate owners of Beck's Grove, Sion Hill, and Constitution Hill. During the 1930's those logs cost approximately ten cents a foot.

After purchasing the logs, Peter had them transported to his shop, where the curing process began. The logs were sawed down to the desired lengths or sizes and left outside in the yard to "cure" for about two years. Curing is the process of drying out the logs or sawed-off pieces of wood so that the air can pass through, under, and around them, causing the natural moisture in the wood to evaporate. When the wood was cured, Peter would cut them up into smaller pieces, so they would be easier to handle.

The milling of the lumber was done by Peter, his foreman Robert Innis, and several apprentices. Milling is taking the lumber and having it sawed, planed and sandpapered so that the wood can be put together for the different types of furniture. The milling work took many long hours to complete. Before beginning his projects Peter drew sketches of the furniture he planned to make, or he would make templates out of cardboard or thin pieces of wood.

His son Peter Jr. (Pete) in an interview, stated that from the time he was 12 years old he did most of the millwork. "One day, my father told me that I will have to learn to use the table saw. So he showed me a box that I was to stand on to reach the table in order to cut a piece of wood as practice. And after that I was doing millwork, sawing down mahogany logs, and turning them over to the foreman."

Peter Thurland Sr. used the mortise and tenon method because he found that technique to be more effective than using nails or screws, which would split the wood. That method was used on the joints of chairs, those parts of the chair that are put together with the back of the chair. The tenon is shaped with an angular edge so that it is glued into the mortise. The slanted tenon will not slip out of the mortise section of the chair or table. Peter never used nails in any of his furniture.

In the early years, Peter used hide glue with the mortise and tenon joints. The hide glue was made from cow heel. Peter boiled the cow heel flakes and then put the solution onto the joints. The glue held the furniture together for decades. Peter also used a glue, which was manufactured in the Orient that he purchased at Clindinen's Store on King Street, the site of the Alexander Hamilton Store and later the Little Switzerland store.

Peter used the dovetail joint style to attach the legs and the paws to the pillar or centerpiece of tables. The dovetail style was much stronger than doweling or making a straight tenon.

Most of the turnings for the pillars were done on the lathe. The Queen Anne furniture style was used because clients liked the foot, the part that resembled a lion's claw and was referred to as paws. Sometimes Peter and his workers had to duplicate the style in wood because the brass fitting paws were not available on St. Croix, or the sizes did not fit properly, or they had a completely different design.

After turning the pillar on the lathe, Peter used a gouge (a curved blade chisel), a plane and chisels to carve the legs. Carving chisels were of different sizes, generally thinner and easier to handle than the common chisel. Some of the carving chisels had curved points, while others had flat points.

When furniture came to the workshop to be repaired, Peter observed the condition of each item. If the furniture appeared to be discolored, he would determine which stain had to be used to bring back the original color or a close match. Sometimes he had to mix one stain with another to get the desired results. After that, the next process was sandpapering by hand.

The hand polishing was the last step. The polish consisted of ground flaked shellac mixed with alcohol. It was placed in a bottle and shaken up until a liquid solution was formed. Then it was poured onto the polishing ball. The ball, a piece of linen cloth rolled into the shape of a ball, was rubbed on the furniture. This process was known as French polishing.

Nowadays, lacquer and varnish are used to shine furniture because French polishing is very labor intensive, tedious, and it takes hours and hours of rubbing to get the desired sheen. It is also difficult to get the ball inside the edges of square items like trays. To avoid this difficulty, Peter would polish the base of the tray and the strips separately, and then glue them together.

A large amount of repair work involved the caning or strawing of chairs. Caning was used as a substitute to having the seats and backs of chairs in slots made of hard wood, which would be uncomfortable for the sitter. Also, the cane allowed for ventilation in the tropical climate.

There are two types of caning. The first and most popular type consists of the weaving of strands of cane through drilled holes in the wood frame to form a hexagonal pattern. It takes about two work days to straw a chair and bind the edges. The second type of caning involves the use of factory woven straw. The prepared weave is knocked into the groove on the chair seat or back, and then a spline is put in place so that the edge of the straw will be hidden and not loosen.

Because of his quality craftsmanship, Peter was given many jobs to do for the St. Croix Municipal Council. He did good work and was the only joiner on the island who did inlay work. Peter made inlay designs with pieces of sandalwood, thibet and mahogany. He made mantles and gavels for the Council and later for the Virgin Islands Legislature.

Peter's eldest son Will Thurland remembers when coffins were made in his father's workshop. "These were always requested about two days before a funeral. Some people wanted the coffin made with a raised roof, while others wanted a glass at the top so that when the lid was opened you saw the deceased's face. Welfare coffins ordered by the government, were constructed with ordinary pine and had a flat top. Peter Thurland added his personal touch by inserting cloth inside to make the box look presentable. Even poor people got a fine coffin from Thurland's Cabinet Shop."

During the 1930's, Peter made furniture for Government House in Christiansted. Visiting dignitaries from Washington, D.C. received mahogany "keys to the city" made in Thurland's Cabinet Shop. Peter was extremely proud of the work he did for two United States presidents who came to visit and inspect the islands. In

1934, he designed and made an inlay table for President Franklin D. Roosevelt. That table was later put on display in the Roosevelt's Hyde Park Museum in New York. The Municipal Council commissioned Peter to make a mahogany desk for the 1948 visit of President Harry S. Truman. Peter built a kidney-shaped desk and inserted tiny inlay pieces of wood in it.

Peter made the bar and a mahogany vase for the Comanche Hotel, as well as other mahogany articles for several businesses throughout the island. One of his Planter's Chairs is on display in the master bedroom of the Estate Whim Museum.

Peter, in the 1930's, did the designs and carvings for the Mother of Perpetual Help Altar for Holy Cross Catholic Church in Christiansted. He was assisted in this project by his sons Will and Pete. Thurland's Cabinet Shop was commissioned to make the benches, pews, and altar railings for Holy Cross Catholic Church. Peter and his sons Will and Pete crafted the confessional boxes, which were made in the workshop and later assembled in the church. Even though the mahogany altars, benches, and pews were taken out when the church underwent extensive renovations in the 1970's, the Mother of Perpetual Help Altar and the confessional boxes were kept and are still in mint condition almost almost 80 years after they were made.

34. The Mother of Perpetual Help Altar, Built in Thurland's Cabinet Shop
The altar is located in the Holy Cross Catholic Church in Christiansted,
St. Croix. Photo by Kenneth Christopher   Courtesy of Karen C. Thurland

Competition with other Christiansted joiners, such as
Victor Solomon and his brother, and Ludvig Harrigan, was
keen. Hubert Jacobs also had a joiner shop in Christiansted.
Joiners had their own designs and styles and could tell the
furniture they made by the various carvings or engravings.

Pete, at the age of 13, assisted his father with wood carving.
He explained, "Those technical parts for the wood carving
you couldn't polish so easy with your hands. So we had to

go to the Apothecary, which used to be Boye's Drugstore, and buy sandra and galliper. Then we mix them with alcohol so that they were thick enough to use to go between the grooves of the carvings. We would use a brush to rub it on because our hand couldn't get between the grooves. As a wood preserve, we used permarganate of potash. We got the powder and mix it with water and it became a purplish color. Then we put that mixture inside the cabinets to prevent termites from eating the wood."

Pete remarked that when his father Peter Sr. worked at the carpenter's shop at the Bethlehem Sugar Factory, Mr. Luddy Johansen asked him to make a Planter's or Lazy Man's chair. "Johansen said, 'Well, I am a short man, so you have to make it my size.' So my father drew the plans for a short person and also for a tall person. Johansen had my father make several chairs for some of the people who were leaving the Virgin Islands Company. Most of them went back to Puerto Rico and to the States.

After the 1928 hurricane, most of the thibet trees started to dry out, and the government had him to cut them down. So he cut them down and used the wood to make the Lazy Man's chairs. Because those trees could stand the dry weather, we never put any finish on them. The way those chairs were constructed they couldn't fall apart because the dowels we used was from imported wood from Tortola called capa. We never used the conventional dowels. We always built our own dowels and used them on hard wood. On soft wood we wouldn't use dowels because they would burst the wood.

Pete recalled that 15 airplanes came and landed at the Estate St. John's airport during the early years of the Second

World War. "My father had to do some work for Lieutenant Storke, who was in charge of the 40th Fighter Squadron. He built a mahogany bedstead and shipped it to Storke's home."

On the subject of bedsteads, Pete remarked that Thurland's Cabinet Shop refurbished one of the bedsteads for the Lord God of Sabaoth Lutheran Church in Christiansted. "There was one bedstead we worked on that Governor General Peter von Scholten used to sleep on. It was very large, and the bedposts were pretty heavy. One of the parsons took that bedstead when he left the island."

Thurland's Cabinet Shop, from its beginning in the 1920's until the 1950's, took in young apprentices. This practice of teaching young boys a trade and having them work for little or no pay had existed for centuries in the Caribbean, the United States, and Europe. Parents came to the Cabinet Shop and asked to have their child learn the trade. Boys from the age of 12 and up worked as apprentices sawing down marked logs, cleaning pieces of work which came to be repaired, and sandpapering pieces of wood. Later they would advance and be involved with the actual repair of furniture pieces.

Many young men received training at Thurland's Cabinet Shop under the watchful eye of Peter G. Thurland Sr. Several of Peter's apprentices became successful in life and made contributions to the community. Others moved to the mainland United States and several returned to thank him because they were able to make a comfortable living in the profession he had trained and encouraged them in pursuing.

The following is a list of some of the apprentices who worked after school and on Saturdays in the workshop:

Claude Berry	Theodore Bostic	Bien Brignoni
Hulbert Christian	Owen Christian	Vernon Ellis
Gene Emanuel	Malcolm Evans	Axel Ferdinand
Stephanos Grant	William S. "Bill" Harvey	Christian Horsford
Darwin King	Joseph King	Clinton Lang
Johnny O' Neal	Lionel Roberts	Leslie Rouss
James Sealey	Albert Sheen	Wayne Thomas

Alfredo Johannes aka Dr. Josef Ben Jochanan

Malcolm Evans, one of Peter Thurland's young apprentices, inquired about payment for work done in the workshop. Historically, apprentices learned a trade and were not paid any wages for the knowledge and experience they acquired in a workshop. Evans remarked, "Mr. Thurland explained that he would not get paid and then told him, 'Let your heart rejoice at what your hands have done.'"

During World War II (1941-1945) young women also worked in the workshop caning chairs and polishing furniture. A few of the women who worked there were Hilda Muckle, Magdalene Phillipus, and Olive Parris. Pete remembered that in the 1940's there were several women who came to his father's shop and said that they used to work in Mr. Barnes' shop in Antigua. Pete remarked, "Those women knew how to do wood finishing."

Will Thurland has never forgotten his father's words:

When you see a tree,

A tree in the forest.
You cut down the tree.
You take the tree out of the forest.
You take the tree to your workshop.
You cut the tree to whatever size
and shape you want.
You create a piece of furniture.

In an interview for *All Ah We*, a student magazine, Peter Thurland Sr. stated, "I have taught quite a lot of people. I spent over 20 years with the Department of Education teaching manual arts, and I also taught industrial arts at the High School. One of my star pupils was Melvin Evans, former Governor of the Virgin Islands. Sometimes, I worked till 2:00 in the morning in order to make ends meet." When the students asked him how long it took to complete one of his chairs Peter Thurland Sr. looked at them with a smile and a twinkle in his eye and told them, "I exercised patience and worked on things."

The creative work of Peter G. Thurland Sr. will survive for future generations to appreciate. His work testifies to the skill and patience of a master craftsman who spent hours perfecting his trade and teaching others how to make fine Mahogany furniture.

35. A Thurland Mahogany Rocking Chair
Photo by Kenneth Christopher Courtesy of Karen C. Thurland

36. A Thurland Mahogany Table with Inlay Designs
Photo by Kenneth Christopher Courtesy of Karen C. Thurland

37. Robert Innis, Foreman, and Peter G. Thurland
Sr. outside of Thurland's Cabinet Shop
Robert Innis was the uncle of Roy Innis, the Executive Director of
the Congress of Racial Equality (CORE). Photo by Will Thurland

38. Peter G. Thurland Sr. Holding a Mahogany Tray with Inlay Designs
Virgin Islander 1979 Fair Use

39. Peter G. Thurland Sr. Observing His Grandson Jean
Andre Thurland Caning a Mahogany Rocking Chair
Virgin Islander 1979 Fair Use

The joinery work had been carried on by Peter's sons, Will, Peter Jr. and Albert (all deceased) and also his grandson Gotfred (deceased). George, Jean Andre and former senator Michael Thurland are carrying on the family tradition. Even Will and Peter Jr.'s daughters have tried their hands at caning and polishing chairs.

Peter G. Thurland's musical career did not end when he left the U.S. Navy Band. He organized the St. Croix Community Band in 1938 and was its conductor until late 1967 when he retired, and his son Will became the conductor of the band. The Community Band played in military and festival parades and held concerts in the Christiansted and Frederiksted bandstands. The community was treated to classical and Popular tunes of the day. Will Thurland remembers the band going to Grove Place on Fleming's or Charlie Clarke's bus to play for the Bull and Bread festivities. Besides playing the popular songs of the day the Community Band wowed the crowd when they played such quelbe songs as "Queen Mary," Fire Down Deh," "Seeley Bells," and "Do My People Do."

The band first rehearsed at the Steeple Building until the government converted that building into a school. Weekly rehearsals were then held at a building which Peter rented on King Street, the site of the former Bank of Nova Scotia near the Old Well. Another rehearsal site was in the building across the street where the First Bank stands today. The band later rented space at No. 58 King Street where the Anchor Inn was located. That building was rented from Charles "Charlie" Richardson for $4.50 a month from 1943 – 1945. Over the years the band practiced in Peter's living room on Hospital Street and at No. 9 New Street, a building he owned in Free Gut.

40. The St. Croix Community Band at Their First Frederiksted Concert in 1938 Left to right, Charles "Charlie" Clarke, Bernard Christian, Roy Peebles, Thomas Martin, Christopher George, Will Thurland, Urban Petersen, Charles Russell, Albert Giroux, Arnold Moorehead, Daniel Baird, Arnold O' Reilly, Peter Thurland Jr., Theodore Bostic, Ivan James, and Peter G. Thurland Sr., Conductor. Photo by Axel Ovesen Courtesy of Will Thurland

Pete Jr. stated, "When we played in Frederiksted, we would go to Amphlett Leader's home and play a few numbers before we came back up to Christiansted. Amphlett Leader had liked the march, 'Thunderer,' and we always played that for him so that he knew that we were in Frederiksted."

Pete proudly stated that his father was an instrumentalist who would go to the piano and trump out everyone's part. "He transposed everybody's part. He was an instrumentalist. Everybody he taught music to he played along with them. If he taught trombone, he played the trombone. If he taught trumpet or alto bass baritone, he played those instruments."

41. The St. Croix Community Band in a Christmas Festival Parade
Left to Right, Peter G. Thurland Sr., Rhudel Phaire,
James Sealey and Ogese McKay.
Photo by Fritz Henle Courtesy of Fritz Henle Estate

42. The St. Croix Community Band at a Donkey Race

Left to right, Peter G. Thurland Sr., Conductor, Robert Innis (tuba), Claudius Henry (saxophone), Albert Sheen (clarinet), Will Thurland (clarinet), James Sealey (baritone), Criminatus "Crimmie" Andersen (trumpet), Christopher George (clarinet), John Sheen (trumpet), and Arnold Moorehead (drums). Courtesy of Will Thurland

43. The St. Croix Community Band Leading a Church Procession
Photo by Axel Ovesen   Courtesy of the St. Croix Landmarks Society

It was a proud time for Peter G. Thurland Sr. when he led the St. Croix Community Band down King Street and up Company Street in Christiansted for the Semi-Centennial Parade in 1967, commemorating the 50th Anniversary of the transfer of the islands to the United States. Many Virgin Islanders, who came down from the United States, gathered at his home at No. 1 Hospital Street before and after the parade to meet and greet Peter's family and the friends who had come over from St. Thomas.

Peter Thurland Sr. received several commendations during the later years of his life and is still spoken of highly by many people today. In 1972, the Alexander Hamilton American Legion Post No. 85 recognized him as a charter member and made him a lifelong member. The St. Croix Community Band held a Grand Concert on June 18, 1976, honoring Peter as the band's founder and first conductor. The Virgin Islands Golden Age Society, at its First Annual Community Leaders Recognition program held on June 15, 1981, honored him for his accomplishments, for his work with youngsters, and for starting the St. Croix Community Band.

Peter G. Thurland Sr. passed away on March 18, 1984, at the age of 92, after a brief illness. His funeral service was held at the Holy Cross Catholic Church, and his body was laid to rest in the Christiansted Cemetery next to his wife Ruth Simmonds Thurland, who had preceded him in death. Several years later the American Legion Post No. 85 laid a memorial tombstone on his grave.

In 1992, Senator St. Clair N. Williams of St. Croix, a former Community Band member, introduced a resolution to petition the United States Congress to authorize the National Park Service to name the Christiansted Bandstand in honor of Peter G. Thurland Sr. Honorable Ron De Lugo, the Virgin Islands Delegate to Congress, worked to get the bandstand named for the man who, as a member of the United States Navy Band, helped to build that pavilion and for over thirty years conducted the St. Croix Community Band's concerts on that same site. Having the bandstand named in his honor would have been a fitting tribute to a man who loved music and shared his musical talents with young people and the community.

When it became apparent that the National Park Service was not going to change its policy of not naming buildings or structures within the National Parks, Sam Bough, assistant to the delegate, got them to agree to have a commemorative plaque placed on the bandstand. As of this date, 2018, no ceremony has been held for Peter G. Thurland. Perhaps, future legislators will take on this endeavor.

Other notable joiners were Samuel Utendahl from Watergut, Hubert Jacobs, Ludvig Harrigan, and the Simmonds brothers. Today, Carol Spanner continues the tradition of making fine furniture and other items from local wood.

AUTHOR'S NOTES

M y research on several of St. Croix's tradesmen resulted in a vast amount of information on various individuals and their work. It was an original plan to include an adventurous fisherman, who had great stories such as being lost at sea, but he moved off island before I could catch up with him. I guess he was the one who got away.

Several people I have spoken to throughout this writing project were very excited and eager to assist by providing names and talking about the artisans they knew in their neighborhoods. Cleoda Hansen Moorhead assisted me with the names of a few fishermen from the Gallows Bay neighborhood. She remembered Ronald Tutein, Edgar Hodge, Hypolite Brunstorff, her father Benhardt Hansen, and her brother Theodore "Chino" Hansen. Cleoda also mentioned that she heard that many years ago Gallows Bay had a blacksmith by the name of Abraham Seeley.

Brenda Henderson spoke about such fishermen as Warner Rasch, Henrique Bastian and Lambert Martin, all from Gallows Bay. She remarked that Eulalie Lawrence and Agnes Paulus were great cooks from that neighborhood.

Larry Finley remembered the fishermen from Watergut such as Arthur Frederiksen, John Charles Thompson, Phillip Turbe, Norman Finley, Isaac Porter, Rudolph Woodrup and Edward Giddins. The bakers were Maude Miranda,

Anne Copemann, and Eulalie "Miss Lee" Callwood. Other prominent Watergonians were Fritz Hennemann, the prison warden; Joseph Foy, a blacksmith; and Harry Edwards, a pharmacist who had a drugstore in that neighborhood.

Finley reminised that the town of Christiansted had engineers like Fritz Tutein and Christian Miller. Also, Roy Sealey was an electrical engineer and the plumbers were Vernon Ellis, Elon Hodge and Rudy O' Reilly.

Alice Cartier recalled her father Valdemar Cartier was a tailor in Free Gut. The bakers were Elodia and Eliza "Lizzie" Thurland, Alice Petersen, Lucinda and Lorna Petersen.

George "Bagoon" O' Reilly stated that his father George Sr. was a tinsmith and Will Finch worked as a chemist. Both men were from Christiansted's Free Gut neighborhood.

There are many tradesmen who contributed to the economic and social life of St. Croix. The men profiled in this book are only a few of the talented Crucian artisans. Hopefully, future Virgin Island writers will document the men and women whose contributions to our community should be remembered.

GLOSSARY

Anvil	A heavy iron block on which heated metal is shaped by hitting it with a hammer.
Appraiser	A person who estimates the quality, amount, size and other features.
Apprentice	One who is learning a trade by practical experience under skilled workers.
Artisan	A person manually trained in making a particular product.
Awl	A pointed tool for making holes in wood or leather.
Bagasse	The fibrous pulp remaining after the cane juice has been extracted. Mixed with molasses for cattle fodder or dried and used to stroke fires in sugar factories. Also known as cane trash.
Band saw	A type of powered saw that is used especially for making curved cuts in wood.
Bajan	A native of the island of Barbados.
Bedstead	The frame of a bed.
Bellows	A device that produces a strong current of air when its sides are pressed together.
Blacksmith	A person who makes or repairs things made of iron, such as horseshoes.
Braze	To join two pieces of metal together using a hard solder with a high melting point.

Buff	A polishing implement covered with a soft material, such as velvet.
Burgher Brief	A license to carry out certain trades and professions in the Danish West Indies.
Burnish	To make smooth or glossy by rubbing.
Cabinetmaker	A craftsman who specializes in making fine articles of wooden furniture.
Chippendale	A style of furniture characterized by flowing lines, sculptured ornately carved shells, leaves, and scroll forms that appear on many decorated pieces.
Congressional Hall	The meeting place for the St. Croix Municipal Councils, Tea Meetings and Monroe Clendenen's Old Year's Night dances.
Coolie	An unskilled Oriental laborer.
Cowhide	The leather made from the hide or skin of a cow.
Craftsman	A skilled worker who practices a craft.
Cricket	An outdoor game played with bats, a ball, and wickets by two teams of 11 players each.
Dovetail	A fan-shaped tenon that forms an interlocking joint when fitted into a mortise.
Dowel	A pin or peg that is used for joining together two pieces of wood, metal, or plastic.
Farrier	A person who shoes horses.
Forge	A place where objects are made by heating and shaping metal.
Gingerbread	A decorative feature. The carved designs used along the roof ledge and balconies.
Goldsmith	A tradesman who deals in gold articles.
Gouge	A chisel with a curved blade.
Great House	The planter's or manager's house on the estate. Also called the Big House.

Hass	Crucian word for horse.
Hepplewhite	An English style of furniture of the late eighteenth century. Chairs were made with square tapered legs and oval or shield backs.
Inlay	To set into a surface to form a design.
Jeweler	A person who makes, repairs, or deals in jewelry.
Joiner	A carpenter who constructs articles by joining pieces of wood.
Kerosene pan	A square pan that contained a thin oil distilled from petroleum. This pan was used by Queble musicians and washer women.
Lard	The strips across the two side rails on a mahogany bed to hold the spring for the mattress.
Last	A block or form shaped like a human foot used in making or repairing shoes.
Lathe	A machine in which a piece of wood is rotated about a horizontal axis and shaped by a fixed tool.
Lift	One of the layers of leather, rubber, or other material making up the heel of the shoe.
Lignum Vitae	A tropical tree having evergreen leaves and heavy sturdy wood.
Linseed oil	A yellowish oil used as a drying ingredient in varnishes.
Madras	A cotton cloth of fine texture, usually with a plaid, striped, or checked pattern.
Mahogany	A tropical tree known for its hard, reddish-brown wood.
Mek	Make
Mortar	A mixture of cement or lime, calcium oxide, with sand and water used in building.

Mortise	A rectangular cavity in a piece of wood prepared to receive another piece of wood called a tenon.
Milling	A slow, tedious or mechanical process.
Newel	A post that supports a handrail at the bottom or at the landing of a staircase.
Permarganate	A potassium compound. When dissolved in water, becomes a pink or purple solution.
Phaeton	Any of various light four-wheeled horse-drawn vehicles.
Plane	A carpenter's tool with an adjustable blade for smoothing, shaping and leveling wood. Planes have different names according to their sizes and uses. There are jack planes, long planes, smoothing planes, rabbet planes, and round planes.
Polish	To make smooth and shiny by rubbing or chemical action.
Potash	Potassium carbonate from wood ashes.
Quelbe	The official music of the Virgin Islands.
Queen Anne	A style in English furniture design known for its curved lines and cabriole (S-shaped) legs. This style dominated furniture design through much of the eighteenth century.
Sandalwood	A tree known for its yellowish wood.
Seamstress	A woman who sews, especially one who makes a living by sewing.
Shaft	The handle of any of various tools or implements.
Shellac	A thin varnish made by dissolving shellac flakes in alcohol and used as a wood coating, sealer and finish.
Shod	Furnished or equipped with a shoe.
Shoemaker	One who makes or repairs shoes.

Soccer	A game played on a rectangular field with net goals at either end in which two teams of eleven players each maneuver around a ball mainly by kicking or butting or by using any part of the body except the arms and hands in attempts to score points.
Sole	The undersurface of a shoe or boot.
Spline	A thin strip of wood.
Stevedore	A person employed in the loading or unloading of ships.
Tailor	A person who makes, repairs, and alters garments such as suits, coats, and dresses.
Taps	A military bugle call or a drum signal sounded at military funerals and memorial services. The official military version is played by a single bugle or trumpet.
Tee-toe-top	A wooden top with four sides played in games of chance. The top was marked on four sides with the following inscriptions: *ALL, PUT, HALF, NONE.*
Tek	Take
Tenon	A projection on the edge of a piece of wood shaped for insertion into a mortise.
Thong	A narrow strip of leather or other material used for binding or lashing.
Tongs	A grasping device consisting of two arms joined at one end by a pivot or hinge.
Trade	An occupation, especially one requiring skilled labor.
Trowel	A flat-bladed hand tool for leveling, spreading, or shaping substances such as cement or mortar.

Unicameral	Having or consisting of a single legislative chamber.
VICORP	The Virgin Islands Corporation, which operated the sugar industry on St. Croix, and electrical plants and ports on St. Thomas and St. Croix, was chartered in 1948 and terminated in 1964. Sometimes written as VICorp.
Vise	A tool that is usually attached to a table and that has two flat parts that can be opened and closed by a screw or lever in order to hold something (such as a piece of wood) very firmly.
Welt	A strip of leather or other material stitched into a shoe between the sole and the upper (leather).
Wicket	A batsman's innings, which may be terminated by the ball knocking the bails off the stumps.

References

Abel, O'Neal. Christiansted, St. Croix. Interview, 22 August, 2015.

All-Ah-We, "Meet Mr. Thurland: Cabinet Maker of St. Croix," Vol. 1, 1974.

Bell, Gloria. Interview. St. Croix, US Virgin Islands, 5 May, 2006.

Brady, John. Christiansted, St. Croix. Interview, 22 August, 2015.

Clendenen, Monroe Jr. Christiansted, St. Croix. Interview, 6 December, 2015.

Dunbavin, Theodora. Retired educator. St. Croix. Interview, 17 August, 1990.

Forbes, Rita. Florida, USA. Phone conversation, 18 November, 2016.

Francis, Hepburn E., "Native Bands in the Virgin Islands." *American Virgin Islands Civic Association Silver Anniversary.* 1956.

Hendricks, Gilbert. Christiansted, St. Croix. Interview, 16 November, 2015.

Heyliger, Cherra. "Hugo 'Nookie' Doyle – The Farrier with the Magic Touch," Flambouyant Park Easter Sunday Racing Program, 15 April, 1990.

Jackson, D. Hamilton. *St. Croix Avis.* "Fellow Citizens Pay Tribute to the Late Peter Thurland." Christiansted, St. Croix, 15 February, 1913.

Knie-Andersen, Bent. *Sukker Og Guld*. Denmark: Nationalmuseet, 2015.

LaBorde, Alphonse Sr. Former Vocational Institute student. St. Thomas. Interview, 19 August, 1992.

Lenhardt, Johannes. Christiansted, St. Croix. Interview, 17 August, 2015.

McGregor, Carlos. Tailor. Christiansted, St. Croix, Interview, 10 June, 1982 and 14 August, 1993.

McKay, Ogese. Navy Band member. Christiansted, St. Croix, Interview, 26 April, 1991.

McKay, Ogese. *Now It Can Be Told: An Autobiography*. St. Croix, U. S. Virgin Islands: Caribbean Printing, 1991.

Rogers, Kathleen. "Interview with Uncle George." *Our Strummo*, V. I. Department of Education, 1977.

Schrader, Richard Sr. *Kallaloo*. St. Croix, U. S. V. I.: Antilles Graphics, 1991.

Schrader, Richard Sr. *Under De Taman Tree*. St. Croix, U. S. V. I.: Antilles Graphics, 1996.

St. Croix Avis. "Charles R. McGregor, Well-Known Citizen, Passes Quietly." Christiansted, St. Croix, November 9, 1960.

St. Croix Source. "Revamped Danish School Opens, Dedicated to Arthur Abel." Christiansted, St. Croix, 2009.

Stockwell, Bruce, "The Craftsman of a Bygone Era," *Virgin Islander*. Tortola, B.V.I. September, October 1979.

Thurland, Karen C. *Peter G. Thurland, Sr.: Master Cabinetmaker and Bandleader.* St. Croix, U. S. V.I.: Antilles Graphic Arts, 1994.

Thurland, Peter Jr. Joiner. Christiansted, St. Croix. Interview, 6 August, 1992.

Thurland, Will. Joiner. Christiansted, St. Croix. Interviews, 1991 – 1994, 2013-2017.

Valls, Lito. *What a Pistarckle! A Dictionary of Virgin Islands English Creole.* St. John, U.S. V. I.: Lito Valls, 1981.

Virgin Islands Council on the Arts. *Arts in the U.S. Virgin Islands.* No date.

ABOUT THE AUTHOR

K aren C. Thurland, Ph.D., of Christiansted, St. Croix, U.S. Virgin Islands, is an educator, historian and author. She is the author of *The Thurland Family and the Furniture Making Tradition, Peter G. Thurland Sr.: Master Cabinetmaker and Bandleader, The 872nd and 873rd Port Companies: My Father's Story, The Neighborhoods of Christiansted, St. Croix: 1910-1970,* and *The Sugar Industry on St. Croix.* She is the daughter of Will and Modesta Thurland of St. Croix. Karen is a 1998 recipient of the Governor's Award for Excellence in the Arts in the United States Virgin Islands.

Printed in the United States
By Bookmasters